WHITEY'S KID

AN AUTOBIOGRAPHY

DR. BERNARD KOIRE

Epilogue by family, including daughters
Alison Brustein & Hillary Lester

 GLASS**SPIDER**PUBLISHING

ISBN: 978-1-957917-24-5 (paperback)
ISBN: 978-1-957917-25-2 (e-book)

Library of Congress Control Number: 2023900301

www.whiteyskid.com

Cover design by Judith S. Design & Creativity
www.judithsdesign.com
Published by Glass Spider Publishing
www.glassspiderpublishing.com

Contents

This book is composed entirely of Bernie's personal writings, which have never seen publication until now. In the process of putting this book together, we endeavored to present the stories in chronological order. Since the entries were written over the course of several years, they include some repetition in order to maintain the integrity of his words. In addition, while we know that much of what Bernie wrote actually happened, we can't verify the truth and accuracy of everything in these pages.

PART I: THREE-BLOCK UNIVERSE

1. Whitey's Kid

I was five years old in 1933 when my older brother Michael and I were exploring the dashboard of my father's new black Ford. We loved pushing and pulling every handle and knob—it was our play tank. Suddenly, the trunk flew open. When we ran around to the back of the car to close the trunk...

"Mom, Mom! We found two dead bodies in the trunk of Dad's car!"

"I told that son of a bitch not to bring his work home!" Mom screamed

Yep, there they were: two dead men. One was shot in the head, and the other had bullet holes through his chest and left shoulder. Curious, I pushed on his chest and blood came gurgling out of the wound. Their bodies were cold and stiff.

Mom spun away from the front door of our brick-faced row house and ran up our wooden staircase to the second-floor bedroom. She woke Dad out of a deep sleep. Before he was really awake, she started in, scolding him about how the boys are now finding dead bodies in the car.

He got up out of bed, mumbling, "They deserved it."

Calmly, he had a couple of cups of coffee. I overheard him tell Mom that he would pick up a friend to help him get rid of the bodies. They would bury the bodies somewhere off the highway in New Jersey where the soil was sandy and the digging was easy. Dad returned late that night. "It's done," he told Mom.

There was a price for being Whitey's Kid. No questions were to be asked. Answers were never offered. "It's done."

"Whitey" was a member of the Jewish Mafia in Philly. To outsiders, it was called Philadelphia - the cradle of democracy. To us, it was our piece of the American dream - two blocks by three blocks in immigrant-laden

Kensington. My father's real name was Herman Cohen, but everybody respectfully called him "Whitey." . The leader of the Philly Jew Gang at that time was Meyer Lansky.

My father was born in the Ukrainian town of Bila Tserkva. For what it's worth, that translates to "White Church." Bila Tserkva is located on the Ros River approximately fifty miles south of Kyiv. The town was founded in 1032. Jews first settled on Ukrainian territories in the fourth century B.C.E. in Crimea and among the Greek colonies on the northeast coast of the Black Sea.

Herman, my father, was the oldest of eight children: Harry, Charlie, Benny, Abie, Fanny, Morris, and Katie. His father, Max Cohen, was an accomplished cabinetmaker and repaired fine antique furniture. He was, at times, called upon to do work for the Czar in the Winter Palace in St. Petersburg, Russia.

Herman was six years old when his parents put him on a Russian freighter as a cabin boy. Although he never had formal schooling, he learned to speak and write eight languages. He knew Russian, English, French, German, Polish, Ukrainian, Yiddish, and Romanian.

He was a stocky, strong, intelligent, and fearless young man. By the time he was twenty years old, he was an accomplished seaman and an officer on his ship. He also had earned enough money to bring his whole family from the Ukraine to the United States. He left the service and, with the rest of his family, settled in Philadelphia.

In the beginning, to earn a living, my father sold fruit from a horse and wagon on the streets of North Philadelphia. Later, as his business improved, he opened a fruit store in the Girard Hotel in downtown Philadelphia.

Not so coincidently, the Girard was headquarters for a significant numbers racket operated by the Meyer Lansky mob. Hidden in the lap of luxury at the Girard, the Jewish mob set up shop circa the 1920s.

Seeing an opportunity to make more money, Herman—now Whitey Cohen—slowly but surely became involved in the "business" of the Jewish mafia.

2. A Taste of Street Life, Kensington-Style

I grew up in Philadelphia in a section of the city called Kensington. It was a poor working-class neighborhood overflowing with immigrant Italians, Irish, and Jews.

Street life in our neighborhood around Albert Street when I was growing up in the 1930s was noisy and colorful. The air was filled with the odor of dozens of competing hucksters in pushcarts—or, if successful, in their horse-driven wagons. The graduates of the street hawking became small shop renters or owners that lined the streets. From seven in the morning to nine at night, this noisy churning of humanity refused to settle down.

"Get your fresh tomatoes," a peddler would yell as he drove down the street in his fruit and vegetable laden wagon pulled by a sorry-looking nag.

Horse droppings were at a premium in my neighborhood. Mothers would send their kids out with pails and shovels to pick them up to be used as fertilizer in their window flower boxes. Every day, you'd see kids getting into fights over who found a piece of horseshit first.

The iceman came in the early morning in a horse-drawn wagon loaded with ice and hay to keep it from melting. He would look at the signs placed in windows indicating the amount of ice a family needed to keep their icebox cold for that day. Sometimes, the iceman would leave his ice pick in the wagon during a delivery, and we neighborhood boys would take it and chip away at the large blocks of ice and suck the shards. They were especially delicious on a hot day.

Paperboys delivered newspapers daily, tossing the morning edition carefully, making sure they landed on the proper steps. Ragmen strolled the streets calling out, "Old rags and clothes! We buy old rags and clothes!"

There were also milkmen who drove in their white trucks, dressed in snappy, white uniforms and caps. They would deliver milk daily to their customers, as well as cream, butter, cream cheese and chocolate milk.

Peddlers who couldn't afford to buy pushcarts had the option of renting them from wealthier businessmen who purchased licenses in bulk and rented them out for twenty-five cents a day, or $1.50 per week.

Troubadours and buskers and dime-store Romeos playing their guitars and singing love songs regularly strolled the streets begging for listeners to put a few coins into a cap held in their hands. They sang, chanted, cried, and laughed in Gaelic, Italian, Yiddish, and sloppy English. Sometimes, a listener from a second-story window would toss a coin that landed in the street, and the singer or his kid would scramble to pick it up.

I could smell the sweet scent of hair tonic if I walked past Connor's Barber Shop on Kensington Avenue. Dad went there every morning for a shave. He had his own shaving mug with his name on it, and his own straight razor which was stored high up on a shelf waiting for his arrival.

In contrast was the garlicky odor coming from the pickle barrels inside Bernstein's Delicatessen. Next door to the deli was the local bar where the smell of beer permeated the air and from where the noise of loud conversation and laughing spilled out onto the street at all times of the day. At night, frequent fistfights would occur there, and the police would be called to break it up and carry away the hotheads in their paddy wagon.

Around the corner on Oakdale Street was a German bakery. From there came the mouthwatering scents of cinnamon, sugar, and butter. The baker was a jolly man with a large black mustachio and beard. He or his wife would give a large free cookie to the kid of anyone who made a purchase.

Often in the mornings, Momwould send me over to buy a coffee cake or some cinnamon rolls for breakfast, and I'd ask for the free cookie with chocolate "jimmies" on it.

In the evenings, under a gas light when the weather was nice, our neighbors across the street would set out a card table under a large sycamore tree, the only one on the block. They sat on orange crates and played pinochle while smoking and laughing.

From time to time, during the day or night from a block away, you could hear the clickety-clack of the els or trolleys as they followed their fixed routes. The chimes from the bell tower of the Visitation Church tolled the hour loudly and clearly, which you could hear from its site on a nearby hill. We would all set our clocks by the chimes from that church.

Every day at five in the afternoon, the lamplighter strolled down the streets of my neighborhood. He would mount his three-step ladder, light the only gaslight on our block, dismount, and continue on his way. Every morning, right at seven o'clock, he cut off the gas, the flame sadly fighting to sputter out.

You could tell time by these reliable workers.

As night approached in my neighborhood around Albert Street, you could hear the radios blaring from each household. The sounds from our favorite radio shows—*The Lone Ranger*, *I Love a Mystery*, or *The Green Hornet*—would be in the air. So went just another day in my life on Albert Street.

3. Sadie the Lady

Her name was Sadie. She was my mother. In all honesty, I know very little about her childhood. Her maiden name was Berkowsky. She was supposedly born in New York City after her father, Mike, and mother, Dora, had emigrated from Lodz, Poland.

She came from a large family. Her older siblings were Morris, who was the eldest, then Katie, Lena, Annie, and Jenny. Then Sadie was born. Her younger siblings were Tessie and Maxie.

The family moved to Chicago, where Mike set up a store across the street from the stockyards making handmade leather boots for the cowboys. I never met my maternal grandparents, but they seemed to be a handsome couple judging by their marriage photographs.

Sadie was tall and slender and loved to dance—and boy, could she. Once, she entered a dance contest at Wonderland Ballroom in Chicago and won first place. She walked away proudly with a trophy for dancing the Charleston.

She cherished it and kept it on the mantel her whole life. Touching it was out of bounds for us kids when we were growing up - she would have killed us for just thinking about it.

On a visit to Philadelphia to visit her older sister, Katie, Mom was introduced to my father, Herman, at a local dance for young Jewish people. Of course, it made so much sense that they met while she was dancing. She never went back to Chicago. After a short courtship and engagement, Herman and Sadie were married.

At that time, my father was working on the circulation platform of the *Philadelphia Inquirer* loading newspapers on trucks. He was eventually fired from his job because of a dispute with his boss.

How would he make a living now? Then he realized there was good money to be made working the streets. He began selling fruit on the street with a pushcart. Soon after, he bought a horse and wagon. Eventually, he opened a fruit store at the Girard Hotel. It was there and then that he got a taste of the underworld of Philadelphia. It was a world my mother hated. The young couple was able to move to a row house on 1840 E. Albert Street. My older brother, Mike, and my younger brother, Lennie, were all born there in the living room. I was born at Temple University Hospital. It was almost a foreshadowing of things to come for me.

As a boy, I remember that my mom was a good housekeeper but a terrible cook. It wasn't until I was older that I found out spaghetti was not noodles and catsup. On a hot day, a typical meal for dinner was cornflakes and milk. However, Mom was a great baker. She made delicious pineapple upside-down cakes.

Sadie gave each of us boys chores to do. I took care of the coal furnace. Mike took care of electrical problems. Lennie did carpentry and painting. My mother was a wonderful swimmer. In the summer, Dad would rent a cabin on the beach at Brigantine, New Jersey, and Mom taught us to swim in the ocean. Sometimes, she would put one of us on her back and swim far out into the waves.

The neighborhood ladies liked Mom. She would gladly mind their kids when needed and organize games for them. She would organize block parties on Albert Street along with Aunt Katie, who was her older sister. They would string up lights over the street and install loudspeakers from the windows for music and dancing.

Life was not easy for Mom with my father being Whitey the gangster. Our family was looked down upon. He was gone often for days or weeks at a time. She would have to bail him out of jail after he was arrested or hide him when the police came looking for him. When he did come home, they often fought.

One day when Lennie and I came home from school and walked through the screen door into the kitchen, we saw Mike sitting at the table and Mom crying. My parents had been arguing, and Mom was set to pour a kettle of boiling water on him. Dad pushed the kettle away from himself, and it spilled out on Mom's right arm and chest, scalding her. She was badly burned and carried the scars for the rest of her life. This was just one visible price for living with Whitey.

Interestingly, my brothers and I each had different feelings about our mother. Lenny had unconditional love for her. I thought that she did the best she could. Mike thought that she was inadequate.

4. Home, Bittersweet Home

"Don't wake up the kids," Mom said, as the police rushed through the front door.

My brothers and I pretended to be asleep. The three of us slept together in one bunk bed—Mike on the top and Lennie and I on the bottom, nose to toes.

There had been a murder in the nightclub that my father owned, and he had come home to hide under our bed. The police searched everywhere but couldn't find him.

This happened at my home on Albert Street where I lived from the time I was born on September 29, 1928, when I was nine. Even though everyone in the neighborhood was poor, our neighbors considered us below them because of my father's criminal activities. They just plain wanted us out. Our home was a brick row house built around 1875 for factory laborers who worked in the weaving mills.

Our place was just like everyone-else's—except they feared my father. This was low-income housing built in the 1800s to house the dirt-poor refuse of Europe, the new immigrants of the Industrial Revolution.

It was a narrow small house with two bedrooms on the upper floor, a kitchen and a parlor on the main floor, and a cellar that housed a coal bin and furnace.

Outside, attached to the kitchen, was a wooden shack that contained a sink and an ironing board. The only hot water was that which was heated on a black cast-iron stove. There was no indoor bathroom or toilet.

The toilet was in a shack in the corner of the back yard. Oh, how I hated the cold winters on Albert Street when we would have to brave the weather to use the toilet. The toilet had a cast-iron bowl and seat with a heavy-duty spring and an overhead water tank. When you were finished and got off the toilet, the seat would spring up and the toilet would flush.

I remember when I was very little that I had to hold tightly onto the bowl to keep the seat from springing up and flinging me into the air. Sometimes, it was so cold that I got stuck on the seat and would have to call Mom to bring a warm moist cloth to release me.

When we could, we would use milk bottles to relieve ourselves. They were placed in the kitchen by the outside door, and each bottle was marked with our initials. We were too poor to afford toilet paper, so Mom placed newspapers, Sears catalogues, and old telephone books on a convenient shelf in the toilet shack. The paper had to be twisted and crushed in order to be soft enough so that it wouldn't scratch or cut.

It was a big ordeal to take a bath. We bathed only on Saturday night. We bathed in a galvanized tub in the kitchen.

Mom heated the water in pots and pans on the black cast-iron stove and poured it into the tub. She would have us all undress and inspect us. The dirtiest kid went last. Mom would bathe in the same tub when we three boys were clean and put to bed.

Many years later, when I went back to Philadelphia for a medical meeting, I had a desire to see the old house at 1840 Albert Street. As I was stopped in front of the place, taking pictures to show my family at home, an old man wearing an overcoat even though it was a hot summer day approached and asked, "Why are you taking pictures of my house?"

When I explained that I used to live here as a boy, he kindly asked me if I would like to see the place again.

It looked even smaller than I had imagined. Then he said to me, "There was a rumor that a Jewish gangster used to live here and that he buried a million dollars in the cellar. I can tell you that I dug up the whole damn cellar and there was nothing there."

5. Summers by the Shore (Jersey)

The summer weather on the streets of Philadelphia was stifling hot and humid. Dad first rented a cabin for a month on the beach at Brigantine, New Jersey, in 1932 when I was four years old. It became our traditional escape in the summer.

Brigantine is on an island and very close to Atlantic City, separated only by a narrow bridge first built in 1924 for motor traffic. It was much cheaper to rent a place there than in Atlantic City.

The Lenape Indians (Native Americans) called the beautiful six-mile-long island Watamoonica, which means "summer playground." In 1925, the Brigantine Lighthouse was erected just as a tourist attraction—and it worked. This was, in truth, our very own summer playground.

The cabin was small and one of twenty-five located directly on the sand. There was a tiny kitchen with a refrigerator, a gas stove, and a sink with potable running water. The rest of the cabin consisted of one large room with a long table with folding chairs. At night, my parents set up collapsible cots in that room and we all slept together. In each corner of the room, there was a curtain that could be drawn for privacy in dressing. Although there were closets along the side walls of the cabin for storage, there were no inside toilet facilities.

The twenty-five cabins shared five toilets, five wash basins, and five showers, all outside. Every person had to bring their own roll of toilet paper, bar of soap, and towel for their own personal use.

No matter how primitive the cabin was, we were all delighted to leave the oppressive heat of Philadelphia to enjoy the cool ocean breeze at the Jersey Shore. My parents often invited our relatives and neighbors on Albert Street to join us for a few days or a weekend at the cabin. No one seemed to mind the crowded quarters. Often, our guests would bring along food or soft drinks and beer to share. Some would surprise us with Philadelphia cheesesteak sandwiches or large soft Philly pretzels, which were always a special treat. The men sometimes set up firepits on the sand and barbecue pork ribs, hot dogs, and marshmallows. Everyone pitched in with the cooking of meals, marketing, and cleaning of the cabin.

In the evenings after dinner, we gathered around the firepits for a singalong. Our visiting neighbors, often immigrants, brought their instruments and sang songs from the old countries.

The Russians sang "The Volga Boatman," my father's favorite. The Poles played polkas on their accordions and danced. The Irish, openly sentimental, took out their fiddles and played as they sang the sad songs of "Danny Boy" or "Rose of Tralee."

In the morning, everyone headed for the ocean only steps away. I watched with fascination as my uncle Max floated on his back, smoking a long black cigar and reading the daily newspaper perched atop his huge belly.

It was here where my mother became that excellent, strong swimmer I described. She would carry each of us boys on her back out to the deep waters and beyond the breakers, as we clung to her neck.

In the late afternoon, when we got tired of swimming, my brothers and I, as well as any visiting friends, would cross the bridge to Atlantic City, which was a few miles away. We strolled along the boardwalk passing saltwater taffy stores and getting free samples from the owners. We held out our hats and they threw in a piece or two then told us to run. We spent a fair amount of time trading pieces with each other for our favorite flavors.Only in downtown Philly had we ever glimpsed these sleek skyscrapers and their thirty-plus stories. They were shiny, bright, and new—a few built in the boom of Prohibition in the late 1920s.

The names still echo in my head as the adults, dressed up in their Sunday best clothes, came back with stories about the posh elegance of the best of Atlantic City. Even the names of these new hotels at the beach boardwalk shouted opulent—the likes of the Traymore Hotel, the Marlborough-

Blenheim Hotel and the Claridge.

We walked past the Steel Pier Auditorium and viewed with wonder the billboards advertising the latest attractions: the diving horses, the man being shot out of a cannon, the big band playing that evening. Our parents reminded us that we were too poor to buy tickets for any of these shows. But it didn't hurt to look.

Before heading back to Brigantine we would detour to the town of Margate, about a mile away, to see "Lucy the Elephant," an amazing wooden structure, sixty feet high, in the shape of an elephant.

The month seemed to pass too quickly. My brothers and I were grateful for this summer getaway. For three summers we spent a month in this tiny beachfront cabin in Brigantine. They were the only vacations we ever had while growing up.

6. Three is Enough (or Three is a Crowd!)

You know, sometimes a kid hears adults just talking—yet from the tone and the tension, you got the feeling something was very wrong.

I was seven years old in 1935 when I overheard Mom confiding to Katie, her older sister. She was upset because she had missed two of her "periods." I wasn't sure what that meant, but I knew it wasn't good news or the right thing to be happening.

Here's what I reconstructed from my memory and the truth behind a well-kept family secret.

This part was very clear. She really did not want another child. Herman/Whitey, my dad, was rarely home. She didn't want to go through another pregnancy. She already had three boys to care for.

Katie suggested that she visit Rose Tomaso, who lived over on Oakdale Street. Rose was known in the neighborhood for "helping" women rid themselves of unwanted pregnancies both safely and affordably. Years later, I learned that the fee was fifty dollars—always paid in advance.

Mom took her sister's advice and made an appointment with Rose for an examination the following week. Rose estimated the pregnancy to be at about three months. She advised Mom to go to the drugstore and buy a one-ounce bottle of tincture of iodine and twenty-four tablets of codeine. In those days, one didn't need a prescription for codeine or cocaine or morphine. I went to the drugstore with Mom, but at that time I didn't understand why she needed all the medications.

Two weeks later, she had another appointment with Rose Tomaso. Aunt Katie told Mom that she would take care of two of us boys while my mom was at her appointment. All three of us, my two brothers and I, she thought would be a little too much to handle. So Mom decided to take me with her. I was proud to be included in this mystery trip.

When we arrived at Rose's house, Mom took me to the parlor. "Sit down and shut up!" Those were her last words to me before she disappeared into the kitchen with Rose.

As I sat in the parlor alone, I wondered what was going on with Mom that was so secretive I couldn't be with her. So I passed the time listening to the radio. There were no sounds coming from the kitchen. Mom was in that kitchen for about half an hour.

I didn't realize until much later that on that odd day, my mother had had an abortion. In those days, a "country" abortion was done by inserting a sterile branch of a slippery elm tree through the cervix into the uterine cavity. The branch was sterilized by baking it in the oven for thirty minutes or by boiling it in water. Then the vaginal vault was cleaned with a tincture of iodine. The fetus would usually abort in three to four weeks. There would be slight to severe cramping for which the patient would take codeine. Of course, I don't remember Mom complaining of pain after her procedure. An "urban" abortion included the tools of the trade.

She was one tough lady. She was one lonely lady.

When Mom came out of Rose's kitchen, she didn't say a word about what had happened. She smiled at me and said that I was a good boy. "Let's go over to Aunt Katie's and get your brothers," she said. "Then we'll all have an ice cream cone and go home."

7. Sundays at the Museum

"Mom, would you please pack us a lunch?" I asked. "I want to go to the museums with Mike."

I loved going to museums as a kid. I especially loved the Franklin Institute of Philadelphia. On Sundays, when there was no school or when I didn't have to work, you could often find me there or at one of the museums on the Franklin Parkway, I loved it so much that one Christmas, my parents gave me a Franklin Junior Membership. This membership allowed me to bring one guest free of charge. I always brought one guest with me.

The Parkway was like moving to France for the afternoon. Ben Franklin designed all of inner city downtown to resemble a well-planned Paris! My mother would pack us a baloney or cheese sandwich and a piece of fruit, maybe an orange or an apple, put them in a brown paper bag, and give us each ten cents for a carton of milk. Then off we would go to the "El" station on Huntington Avenue. There, we would look around to see if anyone had left a transfer on the windowsill.

If we were fortunate, we found one, and then we'd be able to ride without paying a fare. The elevated train took us to City Hall, where we got off, walked two blocks, and began our stroll along the beautiful Franklin Parkway. The Franklin Parkway was a horticultural wonder. Along both sides of the road were planted trees and shrubs and flowers from all over the world. At different times of the year, various flowers were blooming, red and yellow tulips in the spring and multicolored roses in the summer.

In the autumn, the trees turned to shades of red, yellow, and orange. In winter, a soft dusting of white snow covered the gardens. Placed along this glorious parkway were four of the great museums of Philadelphia: the Franklin Institute, the Philadelphia Museum of Art, the Rodin Museum, and the Academy of Natural Science. At the end of the Parkway was the Schuylkill River, which meandered on to Valley Forge. Most of our time at the museums was spent at the Franklin Institute. We would always go to the Fels Planetarium there and watch a show about the stars and planets in the heavens.

I loved learning about the different aspects of the stars and planets in different seasons or in different parts of the world. The Institute was a hands-on place, and Mike and I could spend hours pushing buttons or turning wheels or pulling levers to see what would happen.

After we tired of the science museum, we would head on over to the Philadelphia Museum of Art at the end of the Parkway. There, we would run up and down the seventy-two steps in front of the iconic museum that many years later would become famous in the movie *Rocky* with Sylvester Stallone.

The first exhibit hall that I always visited in the art museum was in the basement. It was where children's art was displayed. I was lucky enough to have one of my own works there. It was a sculpture of the head of an Indian carved in an Ivory soap bar. I also loved to see the displays of rooms and their contents, which dated back to the fourteenth or fifteenth centuries. I was fascinated with the halls filled with weapons of war both ancient and modern.

Mike and I would stay until there was an announcement over a loudspeaker saying that the museum was closing. We headed home satisfied with our visit yet looking forward to the next time.

As I grew older, I found the museums to be wonderful places to meet girls. They would mostly be pretty and intelligent, and sometimes a little adventurous. I always liked smart women. The smarter the better. It would be easy to start a conversation by commenting on an exhibit or display. I sometimes made a date to meet them at the museum the following week. I was lucky. They always showed up.

I still love museums and find them to be wonderful places to spend an afternoon. I have been very blessed that, in my travels, I have visited the most famous museums in the world.

8. It Happened Every Easter

For this Jewish kid growing up in Kensington during the Depression, Easter was a very special day. Everyone seemed to celebrate everybody else's holidays.

First, Mom bought new, three-piece suits for my two brothers and me. She bought them at Bond Clothing Stores for $19 each. The suits had one jacket and two pairs of trousers, and Mom expected them to last all year. This was what Bonds was famous for—a special price for Easter and "2 pants suits." We got these new suits every year.

Then, on Easter, our neighbors, especially the Polish and Ukrainians, would color and decorate eggs, which they would display in baskets in the front windows of their homes. The eggs were elaborately hand-decorated and painted. Some had religious scenes of Jesus and Mary, and others had scenes of spring flowers and birds. Others still depicted mountains, rivers, and lakes. There were eggs decorated with paper flowers and eggs with multicolored ruffled paper skirts. Some eggs were blown out, leaving only the shells, which were then carved into lacy patterns. The neighbors all tried to outdo one another in the beauty of their displays.

The most enjoyable thing that we neighborhood kids did on this special day, at least in my opinion, was to epper. How do you epper? First, you hard-boil eggs, but you don't make them too hard because that softens the shell. Mom would hard-boil a dozen eggs for each of us three boys. We liked to use brown eggs because the shells seemed stronger than white eggs.

Then, with our arsenal of eggs in a basket, we went out onto the street yelling, "Epper, epper!"

A group of kids would come together in the street. Each kid would hold a hard-boiled egg in his fist with just a little part of the point of the egg showing. Choosing an opponent, you would then tap the pointed end of your eggshell against the pointed end of your opponent's eggshell as hard as you could. The combatant whose egg didn't crack was the winner and got to take the other's egg.

Again, you called, "Epper, epper!" to attract a new opponent. The person who ended up with the most eggs was the winner.

The mother of the winner got to make a lot of egg salad.

9. The New Tweed Suit

With every Easter, things got more complex—especially for me. As I mentioned before, each year, our mother took me and my brothers to the Easter sale at Bonds for our annual clothing purchase. And then there was the year she chose three tweed suits in a fabric of black, brown, and gray. Like all the other times before, we had no say in the matter.

All three suits were identical. She also selected shirts and ties for each of us to go with the suits. Not only were the suits on sale for $19 each, but the store threw in free alterations. This was a real good deal. We were constantly growing.

On Good Friday, our mother took us boys back to Bonds to pick up our newly altered suits. As I tried on the suit, I admired myself in the store's mirror. I thought I looked very mature and handsome, indeed.

That Saturday, we Albert Street boys were scheduled to play baseball with the Oakdale Street boys who lived a block away. I liked my new suit so much that I wanted to show it off. I figured it would be a great idea to wear it to the ball game. I knew Mom would never approve, so I snuck out of the house and headed over to the Oakdale Street back lot. Much to my disappointment, no one commented on how grand I looked in my new tweed suit.

The game began. In the second inning, I came up to bat. The pitcher threw the ball. *Smack!* I hit a high fly ball over center field. Dropping the bat, I ran like hell.

The ball bounced twice before the center field picked it up. I passed first base and headed toward second. I knew I'd have to slide in to be safe. I dove, sliding on my stomach with my arm outstretched.

Safe!!!

I dusted myself off, quite pleased with my daring slide into second base . . . until I looked down at my new tweed pants. There, on the right knee, was a hole as big as an apple.

Oh, my God, what have I done? I thought, realizing I'd completely forgotten about my new tweed suit.

I dreaded going home, and I stayed with my team to finish the game. The Albert Street boys won, three to one. Now I had to face my mother. What a calamity!

Mom was in the parlor, sitting on our old brown sofa and reading the *Philadelphia Inquirer* when I walked in the house. I stood before her, holding my baseball cap just right to hide the gaping hole in my new pants. Then I slowly removed the hat, revealing the offending tear.

"Sorry, Mom," I said. "It was an accident."

She was furious. She jumped up from the couch and dropped the now-crumpled newspaper to the floor. "How could you?" she screamed. "You ruined your brand new suit! You'll have to wear those pants for the whole year with a patch on them!"

Without warning, she snatched the baseball bat from my other hand and began to beat me with it. As she swung at my head, I tried to fend off the blows with my arms. She swung at my body and legs, and I did my best to protect myself.

"Stop, Mom, you're hurting me!" I cried out.

Aunt Katie, my mother's older sister, was visiting. Upon hearing the screams and cries, she rushed into the parlor and yelled, "Stop! Stop, Sadie! You'll kill the boy!"

Mom dropped the bat to the floor and sank onto the couch, her fury abated. She dragged me to the tailor's the following week to have my pants repaired. I promised her that I would pay for the work with the money I earned as a delivery boy for the American Store, and that was just what I did.

That tailor did a decent job. By the way, it didn't bother me at all to wear those tweed pants with a patch on the knee for the rest of the year— but you can bet that I never wore them to a game again.

10. The Miracle on Jasper Street

My brothers and I all went to H. A. Brown, a public elementary school over at Sargent and Jasper streets in Philadelphia. It was a two-story brick building with a basement that housed the boys' and girls' toilets. The entrance to the toilets was on the outside of the building. In the wintertime, when it rained or snowed, we had to bundle up to go outside to use it.

The school was in the middle of a concrete playground with only one tree on it. On the playground were monkey bars and a flagpole.

My brothers and I volunteered to raise the flag at eight a.m. every morning. Because I could play the bugle, I sounded "To the Colors" while Mike and Lenny hoisted the flag.

My third-grade teacher was Mrs. Abbot. I liked her a lot. She always had a smile for her students. She wore her hair up in a bun secured by a comb and often wore a black dress with a rose print and a white collar.

On her desk in the front of the room, she placed her pencils and pens, her ink bottle and books, and a very large, ornate Bible. But most noticeable of all was a huge bottle of Horlicks chocolate malted milk tablets.

Every morning at the start of class, she popped a tablet into her mouth and commented on its deliciousness. She would do the same after lunch, again when we came in from recess, and again before she dismissed us for the day.

As the days passed and I watched her enjoy the malted milk tablets, I became very curious about them. I had never tasted one, but I knew they were very expensive at twenty-five cents. One day, Mrs. Abbot was called to the principal's office for an emergency. Since it was so close to recess, she dismissed the class early. I hung back after all the others left.

There I was, alone in the classroom with the bottle of Horlicks chocolate malted milk tablets. I had to have them. I started to empty the bottle, I and discovered much to my disappointment that there were only two tablets left.

I put them in my mouth and began to chew. *Ugh!* They tasted terrible, like medicine! I spit them out into the trash basket, returned the empty bottle to Mrs. Abbot's desk, and ran out of the room. When the class met the next morning, Mrs. Abbot was standing by her desk with her arms crossed, visibly upset. "Somebody has stolen my malted milk tablets," she said. "Raise your hand if you are the one who did it."

Nobody raised their hand.

Now she was really angry. "I'm going to make you swear on the holy Bible," she continued. "If you took the tablets, your arm will fall off."

One by one, each student marched to the front of the classroom, solemnly placed his or her right hand on the Bible, and swore that they didn't take the tablets.

Then it was my turn. I put my hand on the Bible and swore as to my innocence, secretly gazing at my hand, grateful it was still there.

For the next several days when I woke in the morning, I checked my right hand to see if it was still there.

It was. Thank God. A miracle had happened.

11. The Poker Game

Once a year, around November, the boys in the neighborhood got together to play a high-stakes game of poker. We were in it to win enough money to buy Christmas presents for our families. The age of the players ranged from eight to fifteen. We were the serious gamblers on the street.

Besides me, there was Jackie Wickes, who lived across the street and was the oldest of the players. There was also Beefy Ferguson, who lived next door to Jackie, and Dopey Wickes, who was Jackie's younger brother. They were just happy to be there and counted in.

The Hannigan brothers, Danny and Charlie, were part of the poker group, too. And I can't forget my good friends Johnny Miller and Big Nose Bobby. All in all, there were about eight to ten of us from Albert Street and Oakdale Street who joined up to win the big jackpot.

Besides money, we also gambled with blackjacks, brass knuckles, guns, and knives. Handcuffs were sometimes anted up, as well as inexpensive pieces of jewelry that had "gone missing" from a local store. Nobody said where these items came from, and nobody asked. We knew that all could be redeemed for cash at the neighborhood pawn shop.

Jackie Wickes, who was the oldest player, considered himself the smartest thug and a general connoisseur of all things gambled. He arbitrarily placed a value on each item to be gambled and wrote the value on a small piece of paper, which he stuck onto the item to be anted.

For example, a pair of brass knuckles could be worth $10, or a ring might be $6. The values could change after each poker hand depending on whether the player who owned the item had won or lost.

Where to hold this high-stakes game was a matter of serious discussion. The place had to be convenient. It had to be safe. It had to be somewhere that we could see any cop coming before he could see us.

The game was usually held at the home of the parents of Father Kelly, priest of the Visitation Church. The Kellys were usually away this time of year vacationing in Miami Beach, where they would remain until March of the following year.

The Kelly house was on Albert Street next to an alley that separated it from the pawn shop on the corner. The house had retractable striped-orange-and-yellow awnings on the two large front windows. There were three wide marble steps leading up to the front door. These steps were also shaded by a wide and long awning, excellent for concealing from the street a view of any hidden card game.

Because there were so many of us playing, we played with two decks of cards. The game started with large bets from $20 to $30. On this particular occasion, I was lucky on the first hand, winning with a full house in spades. I wagered a pair of brass knuckles and won back the knuckles plus a ring and $15 cash. I was again lucky in the second hand, winning with a straight. The game went on for about an hour, with me sometimes winning and sometimes losing.

It was about five o'clock in the afternoon when, from my perch on the top step facing the street, I saw a policeman strolling down Albert Street.

"Cheese it, the cops are coming!" I yelled.

We all dove into the pot and grabbed as much as we could, then ran in different directions toward our homes, cradling our take in our arms.

As I dashed through my front door, slamming it behind me, I dropped the loot on the floor of the vestibule. I looked it over, evaluating the worth of my collection of guns, knives, cuffs, jewelry, and cash. Lady Luck had kissed me on the cheek. It had been a profitable day.

12. Going to the Movies

The closest movie theater to our house was the Star on Kensington Avenue. The price of admission for a child under thirteen was a dime. The price for an adult was fifteen cents. Even though it was during the Depression, people in my neighborhood could afford the pleasure of going to the movies.

Before going to the theater, I would go to Aunt Katie's store where they sold broken pieces of candy in penny bags. You could get a lot of broken candy for a penny.

One could spend an entire afternoon or evening at the Star. There was always a double feature preceded by the Pathé News, which brought news of world events to us.

Then came previews of coming attractions, a cartoon, and a serial that kept us in suspense week after week. These were usually space adventures like *Buck Rogers* or cowboy thrillers like *The Lone Ranger*. At a time of a local crisis like the Pittsburg flood of 1936, you would be given free admission to the movie theater by donating canned goods to a relief fund for the victims.

Wednesday night was "Bingo Night." This was very popular with the patrons because the winner of the game would receive a small electric appliance.

Even though a ticket only cost ten cents, we neighborhood kids would always try to figure out a way to get into the movies for free. Once, I told the box office attendant that there was an emergency at home and that I had to go inside to get Mom. Of course, once inside, I stayed for the whole show.

Sometimes, when a group of us kids wanted to see a movie, we would ante up enough money to buy one ticket. The person who bought the ticket would enter the theater and then go to the back exit, where the others were waiting outside. He would open the exit door just enough for the rest of the gang to sneak in.

On some nights, the Star would allow kids free admission if they were accompanied by an adult. These nights would be announced in advance. Any adult was usually willing to take a lone minor inside to see the show. Then we would all sit together in the front. I loved going to the movies as a child. When I was very young, I saw many films about wealthy people who lived in luxurious mansions or who traveled to exotic places around the world in splendor.

I thought this was pure fantasy. No one I knew during the Depression ever did anything like that. As an adult, I realized that fantasies can come true. Luckily, they did for me.

13. The Bone Crusher

It wasn't unusual for me to get into fights and scrapes with the neighborhood kids when I was growing up. I was pretty strong and liked to fight because I was good at it.

The Philadelphia Police Department sponsored "athletic clubs" in an effort to stem juvenile delinquency. The Germantown Police Athletic Club was my go-to spot. They trained teenage boys in basketball, wrestling, and boxing.

I was asked to join the group because of my boxing skills. It was there that police trained me in the art of boxing. At sixteen, I was six feet tall and weighed 160 pounds. I had a 28-inch waist and 19-inch biceps.

Years earlier, on a not-so-quiet Saturday night when I was nine years old, the Albert Street gang was on its way to the Star Theater when we ran into the Oakdale Street gang. Their members were mostly of German heritage. No question, their parents belonged to the Bund, an anti-Semitic pro-Nazi organization.

The tallest member of the Oakdale boys, Oscar, called out, "Here come the dirty kikes." He wore a German Bund uniform with a swastika armband.

"Get out of the way, you Nazi bastards," I yelled."

Oscar yelled back, "Make me."

Lenny, my little brother, stood closest to him. Oscar ran over and took his glasses and stepped on them. Then he knocked Lenny down.

Kikes! Touch my Lenny? This made me furious. I walked up to Oscar and hit him in the jaw with a right uppercut with all my strength. This broke his jaw and caused two teeth to fly out. The battle was won. After that, the neighborhood kids called me "Bernie the Bone Crusher."

The Police Department and the *Philadelphia Inquirer* sponsored amateur boxing matches among the boxing clubs of the city. They called it "The Golden Gloves." I fought every week.

Boxers were given a merchandise coupon for $15 for winning and $10 if they lost. If we wanted cash instead, it could be negotiated for a smaller amount.

I won every fight. My sudden "wealth" enabled me to go out on dates. Even though I won, Mom was against my fighting because I would often come home with a black eye or a swollen face.

I was chosen to represent the police clubs of Philadelphia for the middleweight championship nationally. The fight was held at Madison Square Garden in New York.

Two police officers accompanied me in a patrol car to the fight. After spending the night in a hotel, they drove me to the arena. The Garden was filled with spectators rooting for their favorite to win.

My challenger was a fighter from New York. We were of equal height and weight. He was the New York favorite fighting in NYC. I, however, was the more experienced fighter.

I knocked my opponent down in the first round. Before he dropped to the floor, he gave me a black eye. He got up at the count of four. The bell rang for the end of the first round.

I was very alert for the second round. He rushed into a right to the jaw and a left to the stomach. He howled in pain. His nose was bleeding.

This combat went on for six rounds. It was brutal for him. The fight was stopped, and I won by TKO—technical knock-out. The Bone Crusher was declared the amateur middleweight champion of the Police League in the United States.

When I was eighteen, I got an academic scholarship to both University of Pennsylvania and Temple University. Because I needed to work after school and Penn was far from my home, requiring two street cars and a subway to get to class, I chose to go to Temple.

While there, I was asked to join the boxing team, which I did. I fought for Temple University for two years until boxing was discontinued as a sport because of the death of two student boxers.

Although my boxing career was over, my brothers and friends in Philly continued to call me Bone Crusher.

14. My Big Brother Mike

My brother Mike was born on October 23, 1926. He was two years older than me. I'm told Mike was born at home in a bed covered with newspaper and delivered by Dr. Simon Ball. The delivery was uneventful. On the eighth day after his birth, a mohel (ritual circumciser) came to our house on Albert Street. There, in front of friends and family, he performed a bris, which, in the Jewish faith, is the ritual of circumcision.

I always admired Mike and looked up to him. He was my protector when I was very little. If a neighborhood bully tried to pick on me, Mike came to my rescue and beat the bully up. My brother was extremely bright in school and was very good-looking.

When Mike went to Wagner Junior High, he was voted the best-looking boy in his class. He was also an outstanding dancer, and the girls liked him for that. He dated a girl who was voted the best-looking in the class.

Mike was bright enough to be selected to go on to Central High. While there, he joined the school's marching band, where he played saxophone.

I envied him for that because he got to go to all of the school's football games. While at Central, he seemed to lose interest in keeping up his grades. I always knew he was smarter than he let on. But he always passed his classes.

When Mike graduated from high school in 1944, the United States was still involved in World War II. Mike joined the Navy and received his basic training in Bainbridge, Maryland. He was assigned to a destroyer escort, which was decommissioned because of its age, and then he was reassigned to a tugboat stationed in the Brooklyn Navy Yard on Staten Island. He applied for submarine service but was rejected because he had flat feet.

When the war was over, Mike went to Deforest Institute in Chicago to study electronics. After finishing his studies, he returned to Philadelphia and joined the police force. In 1952, he quit the police force to accompany our mother when she decided to move to Los Angeles. There, he went to work as an underground helper for the city of Los Angeles.

One day, Mike was doing some repairs on our house on Cloverdale St. and needed some supplies from a nearby hardware store. While at the store, he struck up a conversation with the owner. Both were from Philadelphia. The owner had a niece, Estelle, whom she thought Mike would like, and she gave him her telephone number.

Now Mike was a little shy, so he gave me her number. I called Estelle and made a date to go to the museum. Mike asked if he could join us. After the date, Mike told me that he really liked Estelle, and he asked me if I cared if he dated her.

Not long after they met, Mike and Estelle, who was a bright and vivacious young woman, were married. Eventually, they had two children, Rosa and Steven. Meanwhile, Mike continued to work for the city of Los Angeles and eventually became head of concessions and parking in the Parks and Recreation Department.

While working for the city, Mike decided to go to law school. After passing the bar, he became a public defender, a career move he liked very much. Mike and Estelle were happily married for many years until her death.

After Estelle's passing, Mike renewed a friendship with a woman named in Sylvia, who lived in Miami Beach, Florida, named Sylva. They had dated when they were young while he was in the Navy and stationed in New York. They fell in love again and married, and Mike moved to Miami to be with her.

Through the years, my big brother Mike and I have always been close. When he was living in Los Angeles, we saw each other often. Now we keep in touch almost daily by phone. I love him very much.

15. Lenny, the "Little Boy Who Couldn't Even Talk"

May 7, 1930, was a happy day when my little brother was born at home on Albert Street. Lenny was delivered by Dr. Simon Ball, just like my older brother Mike.

Births at home were not uncommon in those days. Dr. Ball once again lined my mother's bed with newspapers (because the ink on the paper was resistant to bacterial infections). Dad, Aunt Katie, Mike, and I were all in the bedroom during her labor. Somewhere in the middle of all the noise and commotion, out of the blue, we heard, "Mazel tov!!"

Dr. Ball handed the baby to Aunt Katie, who wrapped him in a soft blanket. She jumped up and danced around the room with joy, cuddling Lenny in her arms. Another boy! This made three boys! Herman, delighted at having another son, kissed both Mom and Lenny and then hurried off to work brandishing a box of Cuban cigars.

To some, Lenny was not a pretty baby. He had a headful of blond ringlets and sparkling blue eyes, but he was cross-eyed and bowlegged. He wore thick glasses for as long as I remember. But everyone adored him. He was Mom and Aunt Katie's favorite.

He learned to talk at an extremely early age. His conversation and chatter were incessant. That's why the family nicknamed him "the little boy who couldn't even talk." He was vitally interested in everything around him. He was fascinated with the street workmen, often asking them if he could help. Often, they'd hand him a shovel or paintbrush and joked as he worked beside them.

Unlike Mike and me, who attended Central High, Lenny chose to go to

Northeast High, which specialized in industrial training. He graduated from there with honors.

After high school, in 1947 at age seventeen, he joined the Navy and became an aviation machinist mate aboard the flagship Bonhomme Richard. Lenny loved Navy life. He was in the Navy for a year and a half, then discharged. He was recalled when the Korean War started a year later in June of 1950.

Lenny and I were in Korea at the same time. When I was wounded and recovering in Tokyo General Hospital, he tried to visit me but was unable to because he was called back into action. Lenny was also wounded, having a piece of shrapnel embedded in his scalp. After that, he was discharged from the Navy.

After the Korean War, Lenny, like the rest of the family, relocated to Los Angeles. He became a liquor salesman, went to college, married, started a family, and eventually became the proprietor of a large liquor store downtown at Figueroa and Olympic.

Of us three boys, Lenny was the most like our father—as far as larceny went. He had three "successful" fires in his store, none of which could be explained. He was sued by the fire department for arson. But lucky for him, he was brilliantly defended by our older brother, Mike, who was now an attorney. Lenny was acquitted.

A windfall from the insurance company enabled him to move to Ojai, a lovely resort town south of Santa Barbara, buy a beautiful home there, and open a huge liquor store specializing in fine wines from around the world. He owned a whole city block where the store stood.

Lenny and I always remained close. We talked almost every day. When he called, he would greet me by saying, "Hello, Berrrrn, this is your baby brother calling."

I lost my baby brother, Lenny, too soon. While inspecting a new home he had just purchased, he hit his head on a rafter. This knocked him unconscious. Thus began a bleeding into his brain that several surgeries were unable to stop. I was with him when he died. Goodbye, little brother.

16. Albert Street Memories

It was Friday. That meant fish for the Catholic families, who never ate meat on Fridays. Aunt Katie and Uncle Max owned an oyster house at the corner of Albert and Jasper streets. I recall how busy they always were on Fridays cooking fish cakes, oyster cakes, and oyster stew.

During the rest of the week, the place was used as a candy store where kids could buy penny candy and prize bags. A prize bag was filled with broken bits of candy and a cheap toy that had been manufactured in Japan. Major Philadelphia newspapers like *The Record*, *The Inquirer*, and *The Daily News* were all sold at the store. Around the corner next to the El station was a public bathhouse where a family could shower for twenty-five cents if they brought their own towel and soap. Dad would take my brothers and me for a shower once a month.

Uncle Max, besides owning the oyster house, worked at *The Inquirer*. He had access to all the magazines the newspaper published. He especially liked detective magazines, as did Mike. By tearing off the magazine covers and returning them to *The Inquirer*, he could get a free new magazine.

Also on Albert Street was a home used as a clubhouse for a hunting club. The club was exclusive to men who were over twenty-one and licensed to hunt deer. Around Christmas, the club members went to the Pocono Mountains in Northeastern Pennsylvania and spend two or three days hunting deer. The hunters tied a slain deer to the hood of the car and brought it back to town. They would then bring it to the local butcher, who would dress the carcass and distribute the pieces of meat to the poor.

I recall, for the duration of World War II, the monthly "coffee klatches" that were held at different houses on the street. They were held on Saturday nights, and soldiers stationed nearby would come. They were served donuts and coffee and ham sandwiches. There was always music at these klatches, and the G.I.s would dance with the neighborhood girls to recordings of big bands. No surprise, Mom, who was an excellent dancer, loved to go to these parties.

Every year on the days after Christmas, the families would drag their dried-out Christmas trees to the intersection of Albert and Jasper. There, they would start a huge bonfire, which was supervised by the fire department.

I remember how the Kensington neighbors would celebrate the New Year. They would all pour onto the street at midnight, banging pots and pans and wishing everyone a happy New Year.

I have many, many memories of my boyhood on Albert Street. Some were happy and some were sad. Some were funny and some were scary. No matter what they were, I will always treasure them.

17. The House on 15th Street

Dad's racketeering career was really paying off. In 1938, Dad surprised us all by buying a house on 15th Street in West Oak Lane in the suburbs of Philadelphia. The cost of the house was $8,700. He was able to sell the Albert Street house for $3,000.

Later, we found out Dad had secretly gone to New York City with the plans of the house. There, he hired an interior decorator, and together they bought furniture, rugs, draperies, and all items of decor for the house. Much of the furniture were fine antiques purchased from an estate sale of the Widener Mansion in Elkins Park on 480 acres. A little fishy, if you ask me.

So when everything was ready, Dad went back to New York for a "final approval of the purchases." He took my brother Mike with him. From Elkins Park in Montgomery County, Mike, the decorator, and Dad accompanied a large moving van filled with the furniture back to Philadelphia. They went straight to the Oak Lane section of Philly to have everything installed at the 15th Street house.

Initially, Mom was furious. When she saw the new place so elegantly decked out the day Dad brought the family to see it, she blew up. She was livid that she had never been consulted and loudly accused the decorator of being my father's whore. Later, Mom admitted privately that she loved the house and the way it was furnished. It was a beautiful three-story stone and brick house with a one-car garage. There was a small front lawn bordered with pansies. In the basement, there was a recreation room with a toilet and a storage room where Mom stored gallon bottles of catsup. There was also a room with a gas furnace (no more shoveling coal).

Shortly after we moved in, my grandfather, who was an outstanding cabinetmaker, built beautiful cedar closets in the furnace room. This was where Dad stored his custom-made shirts and suits. No one knew that my father had such beautiful designer clothes or when he had bought them . . . or how he procured them.

The house also had a laundry room in the basement where Mom had an Easy washing machine with a wringer. No more washing clothes by hand in water that was heated on an old coal stove. She had a machine for pressing sheets, too, which was called an Easy Wrangler.

The entrance to the house resembled the round tower of a castle with a pointed turret. A heavy oak door led into an entry mudroom where one could store umbrellas, heavy coats, and other apparel for inclement weather.

There was another door, this one glass paneled, that opened into the parlor, which was only used for invited guests on special occasions, and where we boys were expressly forbidden to sit unless there was company. On the far side of the parlor and separated from it by two panels of glass shelves was the dining room. On one side of the dining room was a door that opened onto a staircase that led down to the basement. On another side of the dining room was a swinging door that led into the breakfast room and then into the kitchen.

The bedrooms were on the top floor. The back bedroom had twin beds and two mirrored closet doors in the corner. This was where Mike slept. Mike never hung up his clothes and let them accumulate into huge heaps. This never bothered Mom, because Dad had even hired a housekeeper for us.

Lenny and I slept in the middle bedroom in one large bed. The three of us shared one big bathroom, a far cry from the outhouse we had on Albert Street. The large bedroom in the front of the house belonged to my parents. It was a beautiful room with a large, ornate, mirrored dressing table. The bed was on a platform and had a gilded and red velvet tufted headboard. I was happy to be away from Albert Street. I loved our new home so much that I didn't even miss the old Albert Street gang.

18. Albert St. Memories: The Experiment

One sweltering day when we were on summer break from Kinsey Elementary School, my buddies Nathan, Stanley, and Fatso, along with Mike, Lenny and me, decided to play a game of baseball.

We had barely started to play on the field at the Goodfellows' Orphanage when Billy Mitchel came dashing toward us. He was quite out of breath and perspiring from the summer heat as he approached, carrying a cigarette butt and a cigar butt.

"Hey guys," he called out, "look what I found at the trolley stop!"

We dropped our balls and gloves and gathered in a tight circle around Billy. He proudly displayed his treasures. The cigar butt was well chewed and wet, but the cigarette was nearly perfect with only a trace of lipstick at one end and neatly extinguished at the other end by what seemed to be a narrow high heel.

Most of the men and some of the women in our neighborhood smoked, as did the heroes of the movies shown in our local theaters. My father was an avid cigar smoker. After dinner, he would light up an Optimo King to relax. If an ash or two dropped on the carpet, it didn't matter. He rubbed it in with his foot until it disappeared. "This will keep the moths from eating the carpet," he would say. My mother was not amused.

We boys thought that smoking was masculine and sophisticated, but during the 1930s, at fifteen cents a pack for cigarettes and cigars at two for a dollar, what kid could afford them?

We eyed Billy's treasures. Would we dare to light up? Yes!

Since I considered myself the toughest and most daring of my gang, even tougher than my older brother Mike, I decided to go first. I took the well-chewed cigar and put it into my mouth.

Billy handed me a book of matches he had concealed in his pocket. I lit the match, held it to the end of the cigar, and took two long drags. As soon as the pungent smoke entered my lungs, I began to cough and choke. I heard a shrill ringing in my ears, and my eyes started to water. My nose began to burn. This was not for me.

I handed the still-lit cigar back to Billy. He took a few puffs and blew the smoke into the air pretending that he was like tough-guy actor Edward G. Robinson in 1937's *Kid Galahad*. We all laughed at his impersonation, but he, too, soon started to choke on the smoke.

We passed the cigar and cigarette among us like Indians at a pow-wow in a circle smoking a peace pipe. All of us succumbed to the tobacco smoke with tearing eyes, coughs, or running and burning noses. The only one who was excluded was Lenny, who was only eight years old. We "older men" thought he was much too young to participate in the smoking experiment.

After our episode with Billy's found "treasures," nobody felt like playing baseball anymore, and so, a little sick, we all headed back to our homes.

When Mike, Lenny, and I passed through our front door, Mom sniffed at us suspiciously—but never said a word. As for me, I learned my lesson that day and never smoked again.

19. The American Store

We moved from Albert Street to 15th Street Oak Lane in 1938. As soon as we moved, Mike, who was twelve at the time, decided he wanted to look for a job.

He found one at the American Store, the local grocery store located at Broad Street and Chelten three blocks from our house. He saw a sign in the window advertising a need for a delivery boy. Although there was no salary and he would have to sweep the floor of the market and keep the pavement in front clean, he would get to keep all of the tips earned by delivering groceries to the customers. Mike applied and was hired for the job.

He decided that he needed a wagon to help him with the deliveries and asked Lenny and me to help him build it. Together, we constructed a ten-by-three-foot wooden platform and attached wheels to it. The Cohen brothers were in business!

We delivered groceries every day after school and on Saturdays. We delivered in all types of weather: in snow, rain, sleet, or the heat and humidity of summer.

Oak Lane was a hilly neighborhood, and it was difficult going up and down those hills. The wagon could carry up to ten boxes and could be quite heavy. Tips were dependent on what customers wanted to pay. They could range from ten cents to two dollars. We gave all of the money we earned to Mom and kept none of it for ourselves.

Sometimes when the weather was cold, a patron would feel sorry for us and invite us in for a cup of hot cocoa and cookies. In the summer, when it was hot and humid, we would be offered a glass of iced tea or lemonade.

In 1941, because of the start of World War II, everything changed. One had to belong to a union to work as a clerk in a grocery store, and the hiring age was lowered to thirteen. Mike and I were both hired as grocery clerks and joined the United Food and Commercial Workers Union. Lenny became the sole proprietor of the delivery business until he was old enough to join us as clerks at the American Store.

We felt lucky to be working at the store during the war years. Since there was no refrigeration to keep the produce from spoiling over the weekend, Mr. Gurley, the manager, would permit all his clerks to take home fruits and vegetables that were still good but in danger of spoiling. We ate well, enjoying the sweet if slightly overripe flavors of watermelon, strawberries, cantaloupe, and honeydew melon. To this day, I like my fruit a little overripe. We also got to take home bread, rolls, cookies, and cakes that had passed their expiration dates.

The American Store was a full-service store. This was before what you would call "self-service" supermarkets had developed. All a customer needed was their shopping list, and we clerks would go around the store to collect the desired items. Not all products were packaged. Cookies and crackers came in bulk. Pickles, sauerkraut, and cider were in barrels. Fruits and vegetables were loose. Cheeses and butter had to be cut to order. Laundry soap was unwrapped and sold by the bar. And, of course, we all had to enforce rationing for the war cause: Only your fair share!

When the patron was finished shopping, we clerks had to list the price of the items on a paper grocery bag and total the amount. There was no adding machine. We added in our heads. A cash register was used only to take in money or to give out change.

I worked at the American Store until I graduated from Temple University. I started at a salary of thirty-seven cents an hour and finished at a whopping dollar-fifty cents an hour, which was a great wage at the time.

20. The Rationing Years

During the years between 1942 and 1946, the United States imposed rationing among the general population because of World War II shortages. Once a month, each family received a book of stamps that had to be used during that month. This really affected the business at the American Store where we worked.

Shopping became quite confusing for both customers and us, the store clerks. In order to buy butter, meats, cheeses, and oils, patrons had to use their red food stamps. When buying sugar, canned goods, juices, dried beans, and frozen fruits and vegetables, our patrons would have to use blue stamps.

It took a lot of extra time to figure out how many stamps were needed and what color to use. We store clerks started to become very casual about it all and just threw some stamps in the collection box. We also had our favorite customers and would sometimes sell them items without collecting any stamps at all.

I admit I took advantage of my position at the store. When I went out on a date, I brought along a pound of butter for the girl's mother. Needless to say, this was much appreciated and made me very popular with the mother as well as with the daughter. Sometimes, I brought a one-pound box of sugar. The mother would *really* like me then. Often, a mother would encourage me to date her daughter again.

I didn't have a lot of money to spend, so a usual date was either going to a movie or to a house party where everyone would jitterbug to the big band recordings.

Even though gasoline was strictly rationed, my friends were able to get around it. I had several who worked at gas stations and filled up the tank of a buddy's car without collecting their stamps. I didn't have a car but always managed to hitch a ride.

We would often head on over to The Hot Shoppe, a drive-in restaurant on Broad Street. You could always count on the pretty young girls on roller skates who would glide up to our car, take our food order, and, with a sunny smile, deliver the order to the car window.

As far as food stamps went, our family was very fortunate. We boys brought home so many overripe fruits and vegetables that Mom began to preserve them in mason jars. She even started to make wine out of rotting grapes, which she stored in two-gallon jugs and kept under the kitchen sink. There was a deep fairness to her. She gave any of our leftover food stamps to the store at the end of every month.

I became friendly with many of the women who shopped three or four times a week at the American Store. They told me about their sons who were in the service. Hoping to avoid active combat, some of their sons had joined the Merchant Marines early on.

Unfortunately, a few of them were aboard transport ships carrying military supplies to England, which were torpedoed by Nazi subs. Other mothers would tell me of sons in other branches of the service, some who were wounded or some who had died. These were called "Gold Star Mothers," and they placed a small flag in a window of their home bearing a gold star honoring the son who gave his life for his country.

World War II ended in 1945, and everyone was grateful. Rationing ended in 1946, and the whole country drew a sigh of relief.

21. The Line-Up

My father was not just a member of the mob. He was a racketeer and owned a few nightclubs in Philadelphia as well as in Atlantic City. He had many employees and was the big "moneymaker" of the family, so all of his brothers looked up to him.

"Harry," Mom shouted at my uncle, "you ought to be ashamed of yourself for coming here and skimming the cream off the top of the milk bottles! The boys need it. They're growing boys. I'm going to tell Herman right now!"

You see, the family had their judgments and expectations of my father—but everybody clearly wanted some of the cream.

It was Monday morning before noon. Like a ritual, on that day of the week all of Dad's brothers came to our house on 15th Street, where they waited in line for him to hand out his weekly doles to supplement their income. Usually, they'd wait quietly for him to get up, but on this particular morning, Uncle Harry's habit of skimming cream really aggravated my mother.

Dad heard the ruckus, which awakened him from a sound sleep in his front bedroom on the second floor. He charged to the top of the stairs clad only on his shorts, hair rumpled and unshaven, the scars on his face blazing. "Can't a stiff get any sleep around here?" he yelled.

On most Mondays, Dad would get dressed at his leisure and come downstairs. All the men would gather around the kitchen table. As they joined him for breakfast, the brothers would tell my father how their businesses were doing and how much money they would need for the week.

Uncle Harry was an actor and an adagio dancer. So he was often unemployed. I remember once taking some friends to watch him perform with his beautiful dance partner on the Yiddish vaudeville stage. I was terribly embarrassed to watch him flit around in his leopard-skin jockstrap-like leotard.

Uncle Benny had a wholesale market where he sold fresh fruits and vegetables directly from local farmers. They said he did quite well, but still came for his handout.

Uncle Charlie was the only college graduate of the bunch. He was also an Eagle Scout and worked for his father-in-law, who owned a haberdashery. He was always elegantly dressed and was gentlemanly and soft-spoken.

Uncle Morris, who did the best (except, of course, for Dad), was in the pigeon business. He raised champion racers, sold pigeon feed and medicine for sick birds, and organized homing pigeon races throughout the country. He became a celebrity in his field.

Uncle Abie was the only brother who didn't come for a handout. He made a career of raising and training horses. He worked for prominent, wealthy estates in and around Philadelphia. During World War II, he was in the cavalry and became the chauffeur for a general. His expertise with horses so impressed the general that he recommended Abie for Officer Candidates School. He entered World War II as a private, and after serving with General "Vinegar Joe" Stillwell in China, he left it as a major.

This "Monday morning line-up" tradition lasted for many years until Dad mysteriously disappeared in 1943. After that, my uncles never even came around for a visit. I was disappointed in their lack of care and concern for their brother's family. After Dad was gone, it was as if we had never existed.

As for Mom, even as a widow, she was glad to get rid of them. She had always said that "they were no God damn good."

22. Central High

"I got accepted to Central High," I told Mom as I opened the letter of acceptance addressed to my parents. Mom was delighted for me. Mike was already a student there. This was in the fall of 1942, and I was ready to enter the ninth grade.

Central High was founded in 1838 and was the second-oldest high school in the United States. When the school first opened, graduates were awarded the degree of Bachelor of Arts. Most of the attorneys, accountants, and physicians who practiced in Philadelphia graduated from Central. The school maintained a quality of academic excellence, and only academic classes were taught there. To be accepted there, one had to be an honor student and be recommended by his teachers. It was conveniently located near us on 1700 W. Olney off Broad Street.

This school taught me to be competitive academically. Since its inception, only boys were allowed to attend. Girls' High was developed soon after in 1848 and was equally competitive. This was even more conveniently located at 1400 W. Olney near Central, and it made it cool to be smart for guys and girls.

Even in this four-year university preparatory magnet school where all students were bright, there were classes offered at the university level for the most gifted students, and I was lucky enough to be selected for these classes. Most of the teachers at Central High were PhDs in their fields of expertise. It was considered an honor to be on the faculty.

I loved going to Central High and meeting boys from all over the city and from many different backgrounds. I was one of the poorer boys in the school. I had to wear my uncle Max's old Army khakis. They were in crisp condition because he received a medical discharge early from the service during World War II. I also carried my books in a repurposed pillowcase that Mom had made for me. Some of the guys teased me about the pillowcase, but it didn't matter. I beat them up, and that would stop the teasing. They soon learned not to fool around with the "Bone Crusher."

Mike had a different experience at Central. He joined the school's marching band playing saxophone. Mom didn't let me join because she thought Mike needed to practice more than I did. She must have thought he was another Rudy Valle. So he got to see all the football games, and I never saw one. I can't say I wasn't a little jealous.

I had some favorite classes and teachers. I loved Dr. Disheroon's Shakespeare English class. He amused his students by reciting all the parts of the characters himself. Years later, he was selected to be in Central's Teacher's Hall of Fame.

Dr. Shock's calculus class was very challenging. He would write a problem on the blackboard, and the first student to get the correct answer got extra credit. Because I was good at math, I volunteered to tutor students who needed extra help.

The highest honor a student could receive was a 10k Gold Barnwell Button. I was given this award for having been a student tutor. At graduation, I received the mayor's scholarship, which enabled me to attend either Temple University or the University of Pennsylvania without paying tuition.

I would have preferred to go to Penn, which was an Ivy League school, but it was quite far from my home. After Dad disappeared, I had to help support Mom. So I worked every day after school at the American Store. Temple University was much closer to home. This would allow me to keep working, so that's where I chose to go.

23. The Palace of My Delights

I was fifteen in 1943. At that time, the object of my affections was Helen Ward, a girl from my old Kensington neighborhood. She was a curvaceous young lady with curly brown hair and a spray of freckles across her nose. She had an adventurous nature and seemed to share the same affection for me as I had for her.

We often went to the movies together at the Star Theater or to dances at the Visitation Church on Sundays, but there was always a crowd. Unspoken, we longed to be together *alone*.

I thought long and hard about where we could be together with complete privacy. I had very little money to spend. The solution came to me one day as I was walking by the historic Palmer Cemetery at 1410 E. Palmer in Kensington, which wasn't far from sweet Helen's house.

The Palmer Cemetery was one of the oldest cemeteries in Philadelphia dating back to the pre-Revolutionary War era. The expansive lawns were dotted with ancient trees that shaded granite and marble tombstones of various sizes and shapes. Monuments to the fallen heroes of our country's wars were placed here and there on the grounds. But what captured my attention was one of the several family mausoleums that were situated along the margin of the cemetery.

I walked over to the mausoleum with the name Cramp carved in marble over the doorway. To my surprise, the metal door of the entrance was open, and I walked inside.

Although the structure was rather plain on the outside with smooth marble walls and a conical slate roof, the inside was glorious. Stained glass windows showed biblical scenes on all four walls, which allowed the sunlight to stream in in all the colors of the rainbow. There were three crypts of ornately carved marble in the center of the floor.

Although beautiful, the place was dusty and cold. There were some spiderwebs on the ceiling, but I was happy to find electrical outlets on two of the side walls. I knew I had a lot of work to do to turn this into "the palace of my delights."

I made a date with Helen the following Saturday evening, and in the late afternoon of that day, after the cemetery had closed to the public, I climbed the low fence surrounding it and began to transform the place. I brought a broom, dustpan, and cleaning rag from home and cleaned the chamber as best I could.

Then I placed blankets and pillows on the floor. I brought six Yahrzeit memorial candles from home that Mom always kept in supply for family remembrances. I placed a bouquet and a box of chocolate candies next to the blankets. Now I was ready to pick up Helen.

Freshly showered with radio and flashlight in hand, I knocked on Helen's door. She was decked out in a full skirt and lacy blouse. I asked her if she was ready for an adventure, and she smilingly said she was.

Helen seemed surprised when we got to Palmer Cemetery and I told her we had to climb over the fence. But she was game and eager to see my surprise. I led her over to the Cramp family mausoleum by the light of my flashlight and asked her to wait while I went inside.

Once inside, I lit the candles and plugged in the radio. I turned to the station where The Hit Parade was playing. Then I brought Helen inside to see my romantic offerings.

I was afraid that she might be angry with me, but she laughed, her eyes sparkling in the candlelight, and she seemed delighted with my efforts. She threw her arms around me and kissed me sweetly.

Suddenly, there was a banging on the mausoleum door.

"Who's in there?" an angry voice called out.

I cautiously cracked opened the door. It was the night watchman. He had been alerted by the music coming from the radio.

After he stepped inside and assured himself no damage had been done, he politely and with a blush asked us to leave.

I slowly gathered up all of the items and gifts I had brought, and we left as quickly as possible. Afterward, we often talked and laughed about our adventure together at our palace of delights.

24. Called Him "Dad"

Herman "Whitey" Cohen, the man I called Dad, was born in Ukraine in 1904. He was a member of the Jewish Meyer Lansky gang. He was a boxing promoter, and along with his partner, Pete Moran, promoted the Joe Louis-Tony Galento heavyweight championship fight that took place on June 28, 1939, at Yankee Stadium in New York.

My father was also a nightclub owner, a gambler, and a bootlegger. After Prohibition ended in 1933, he ran a numbers racket out of an office on 69th Street in West Philly. He was arrested and charged with the murder of fellow Polish gangster Mickey Duffy, but later the charges were dropped.

A man as powerful and dangerous as the Irish mobster Mickey Duffy naturally attracted enemies. During the night of August 29th, 1931, as he lay sleeping in his suite at the Ambassador Hotel in Atlantic City, someone shot him dead.

Whitey was a tough guy, and the men in the neighborhood were afraid of him. My brothers and I loved that. One day, when I was about seven, Dad took me to visit his youngest brother Morris's pigeon store on Third Street. Morris, president of a national society of pigeon owners, was locally well known for the speed and swarming ability of the birds that he sold from his store.

On that day, a disgruntled customer came in and threatened Uncle Morris with a crowbar that he'd picked up off the counter. He was unhappy with a bird he'd purchased for swarming. Dad stepped up to the angry customer, grabbing him by the collar and lifting him off the ground.

"Are you looking for trouble?" Dad asked.

The customer dropped the crowbar and fled the store. I was very proud of the way that my father defended his brother.

Yet, despite his lawlessness and the fear he invoked in others, to my brothers and me, he was a caring and loving father. One night, I was working on a school project on the Panama Canal. I was trying to build a model of the canal out of shirt cardboards.

I was discussing the project with Mike when Dad came over and sat down on the floor next to us. "Let me help you with this," he offered. "I've been through the Canal many times when I was at sea."

He sat with us for several hours, explaining the workings of the locks and how ships proceed from one level to the next to traverse the canal.

The following evening, Dad asked me how things went with the project at school. When I reported that I'd gotten an A and that my teacher said I'd built the best project in the class, he smiled.

"Happy I could help you, son," he said.

I wish I could have known my father better, but I was only fifteen when he disappeared. I admired him for his toughness and for his position as the head of the family including my uncles, aunts, and cousins.

I never considered going into a life of crime as Dad did. Some of the qualities I believe I inherited from him are my love of adventure, my ability to face danger squarely, and my deep love of family.

PART II: BEYOND KENSIGTON – FINDING MY DREAM AND A WAY OUT

25. Whatever Happened to Whitey?

The last time I saw my father, I was fifteen years old. It was 1943, and I was in the tenth grade at Central High School.

We had breakfast together, fried eggs and salami—his favorite. He remarked that he would be out of town for some time on business. No one thought this was strange or unusual. He often would be out of town for long periods of time. This time was somehow different. His absence extended from weeks to months.

In the basement of our 15th Street home, my grandfather had built large cedar closets where Dad stored his many custom-made suits, shirts, ties, and shoes. They were made by the finest tailors and haberdashers in New York City.

Mom was suspicious. So she checked to see if any of Dad's clothes were missing. None were. There was no word from him. We didn't know where he was.

An unmarked weekly envelope began to show up in our mailbox at the end of six months. In the plain envelope was a fresh $100 bill.

Mom contacted Johnny Murphy, Dad's closest friend, to see if he had any information. All he could tell her was that something bad had happened to my father. A large amount of money was missing from the nightclubs that Dad owned in partnership with Meyer Lansky and his gang.

Meyer Lansky had held Whitey personally responsible for the loss. Johnny Murphy simply said that Dad probably ended up "in a barrel of cement at the bottom of the Delaware River." My mother was warned not to pursue it.

Mom was afraid to call the police, but she did report Dad's disappearance to the Metropolitan Life Insurance Company. Years before, she had secretly taken out a life insurance policy on Dad. Each month, she had faithfully paid the premium, and the policy was current. Because of the circumstances of Dad's death, there was no death certificate, so the insurance company would only refund the premiums Mom had paid.

Dad had another close business associate, Frank Polombo, who owned several restaurants, performing venues, and private after-hours nightclubs in South Philly. Palumbo's, Nostalgia's Restaurant, and the Click Club were the places to be seen, meet, get your start as a performer, and hang out with the in-crowd.

In Pennsylvania, state "blue laws" required all bars to close at midnight except for private clubs. I went to Frank's Click Club at 16th and Market, and he welcomed me like a long-lost son. That was the place to be for the best new music. Palumbo always knew what was what in Philly.

I asked Palumbo if he knew anything about my father's disappearance. He said, "Bernie, you can come to my club anytime. There won't be any cost to you. Whitey was one of my best friends. But do yourself a favor, kid. Don't go around asking what happened to him. It's all over now. If you knew any more, it could cause you trouble."

Frank was one of the kindest and most generous people in South Philly, especially to orphans and poor kids—but he was connected. Those were always the rumors.

So we continued receiving the weekly money in an envelope for two years. Then, as abruptly as it had started, it stopped.

Mom seemed rather stoic about Dad's disappearance. Their marriage was a turbulent one, with much fighting and bickering about his involvement with the mob. She was also afraid to start up with the police or my father's past associates.

All my brothers and I knew was that we had to support our mother and ourselves. So quietly we, too, lowered our heads. We continued working at the grocery store. Mike and I were clerks, and Lenny helped in the meat department. We didn't lack for food thanks to Frank Gurley, the store manager, who let us bring home any food that looked like it would spoil over the weekend. He was a godsend.

It was now the middle of World War II, and it was common for women to fill jobs left vacant by men who went off to fight. Mom, on the other hand, never worked. Mike always resented her for it. For a time, she took in student boarders who attended local universities. But this only lasted about two years before she tired of it.

At seventeen, after graduating from high school, Mike joined the Navy and sent his pay home to Mom. That was how we survived after Whitey's disappearance.

Herman "Whitey" Cohen was neither seen nor heard from again. No questions asked.

26. Joe Campbell's Meager Consolation

On one scorching morning in Philadelphia in August of 1945, my friends and I were hanging around the home of our pal Nathan Wolfe. It seemed that every summer was killer hot and humid.

Most of us were about sixteen years old. We were teenage boys with time on our hands. Nathan's family had gone to Florida for the summer, and his father had left the family's car, a '38 Cadillac, in their garage. Bad mistake. Sixteen cylinders and sixteen-year-olds don't mix well.

You see, Nathan had just gotten his driver's permit and suggested that we all drive to the Shore to cool off at the beach. We greeted his suggestion with enthusiasm and hurried home to get our bathing suits and towels. Luckily, we remembered to grab some food to eat along the way.

Nathan drove, and the four of us were soon on our way. Joe Campbell, a six-foot-four-inch high school football player, sat in the front passenger seat. Lennie and I were in the back seat. We zipped across the Delaware River Bridge going east to the Black Horse Pike, which would take us straight to Atlantic City.

Joe, the football player, was recovering from a bad chest cold and was still coughing up a lot of phlegm. He had brought along a box of Kleenex but had, by now, used it all up. We were stopping at a light when Joe started to cough. He rolled down the window and hocked an epic loogie. It was a beaut! It flew at least six feet and was yellow as a summer marigold.

We were admiring this accomplishment when a car pulled up in the lane to the right of us. Almost in slow motion now, the wad lingered. And then it flew, with a little wind assist, through the open window and onto the neighboring driver's face.

The driver of the car was beet-red and furious. He leaped out of his car, grabbing something from his front seat. As he swung around the back of his car, we saw he was waving a tire iron. He was spitting-angry and cursing. Now he was threatening to hit that "son of a bitch - who caught me on my fucking face!"

All six feet four inches of Joe yelled, "Yo, seriously, I'm so sorry, sir."

Joe was still in his seat when the driver started to swing the tire iron. That was when Joe's football instincts took over. He whipped around and reached out with his enormously long arms, grabbed the guy's shirt, and gave him a strong yank. He was trying to stop the guy from destroying his family's car—that was all. But when the guy's jaw hit the roof of the Cadillac, out flew several teeth. We all looked at each other as we heard the crack of his jaw as it broke.

The incident caused a giant, snake-like traffic jam on the Black Horse Pike state highway. Then the New Jersey Highway Patrol pulled up, sirens blasting. They called an ambulance for the bleeding and unconscious driver, threw Joe in the back of their cruiser, and arrested him.

Two sturdy troopers interrupted our explanations. They ignored everything we said. The fact that Joe had been threatened by this guy seemed to make them no mind. Nothing made any difference. They hauled Joe away to Penns Grove Jail.

We headed home. Needless to say, our plans for the Shore were ruined. We had no choice but to leave Joe in jail. We spent the rest of the day and night telling Joe's parents what had happened. They were not interested. We were a "bad influence."

That wasn't the first or last time we would hear that from our friend's parents. Poor old Joe was set for trial the following week. Nathan, Joe's parents, and I drove back to Penns Grove to hear Joe sentenced to one month of hard labor at the prison farm. He would end up picking tomatoes that would be sold to the Campbell Soup Company (no relation).

Two weeks later, Nathan and I visited Joe at the prison farm. We asked him how he was doing.

"It's not so bad," he said. "I'm eating a lot of fresh tomatoes, and the views are spectacular."

"What do you mean?" I asked, looking at the fields of nothing but row upon row of tomato plants.

He said with a dumb grin, "That's why it's called the Garden State."

Damned if I still don't miss that innocent grin.

Joe took Nathan and me by the arm to the farthest edge of the farm. There, across a dirt road, was a white sandy beach glistening by the Delaware River. On the beach were young women and men playing and running on the sand or laughing and frolicking in the river, all stark naked. Ironically, the famous Sunshine Nudist Colony of New Jersey had its private beach right next to the prison farm.

As the three of us stood and admired Joe's spectacular view of the Colony. Two young ladies waved and smiled at us, clearly signaling us to join them. With a sigh, Joe, Nathan, and I turned slowly and walked back to the prison farm visitors' center.

I thought to myself as we left the prison farm that it was really an unfair thing that happened to Joe Campbell. Even being able to gaze upon those lovely naked ladies was no consolation.

27. A Not Very Silent Night

Fa la la la la, la la la la. It was Christmas Eve, and I was invited to the annual Christmas party at Dr. Martin's house. I was a friend of Dr. Martin's older daughter, Mary Ann. Dr. Martin was our family's dentist. Mary Ann and I were both sixteen, and I liked her a lot. She was tall and beautiful and very bright.

The party was held downstairs in their recreation room, and it was decorated elaborately to celebrate the joyfulness of the season. There was a splendid fir tree that reached the ceiling and was laden with colorful ornaments and twinkling lights. Mistletoe hung over the doorway. There was a jukebox playing holiday songs. Everyone was having a wonderful time drinking, eating, and dancing.

Suddenly, the downstairs bell rang, and when the door was opened, Dr. Martin appeared. The man of the house was disheveled. He seemed to have been drinking because he was swaying slightly and slurring his words. He explained that he had been in a car accident and that he had to leave his car at the corner of Broad and Allegheny. He said that he was so upset and nervous that he felt he couldn't drive home, and so he took the subway. He asked if anyone would volunteer to pick up his car and bring it home.

I eagerly volunteered, keeping my eye on Mary Ann to sense her reaction. I'd just gotten my learner's permit and was anxious for any opportunity to drive, but it was illegal for me to drive alone without an adult.

I put my hand out to him, and Dr. Martin handed me the keys to his car, a dollar for the subway, and I was off. I really wanted to impress Mary Ann.

When I arrived at the site of the accident, a policeman was standing by examining a huge dent in the right-front fender. The car was parked in front of an apartment house. As I stood there, an old woman opened her apartment window and yelled out, "Yo, Officer! That's the palooka driving the car and ran away!"

The cop hoisted me off my feet by my collar and shoulder and put me in the squad car. I was taken to the police station, where they booked me.

As I stood in front of the sergeant at the booking desk, I vehemently denied being the driver of the car. *Bang!* I was booked for hit-and-run. Then two cops dragged me to a cell. For effect, they slammed the door shut as hard as they could.

I clenched my fist. My jaw muscles tightened. No matter. After about fifteen minutes, a cop told me that I could make one phone call.

Well, I called the Martin house. Thank heavens the doctor answered the phone. He started apologizing. I let him go on a little. Then I hesitated, took a breath, and told him I was in jail.

He felt terrible I was arrested. He said that he would come right over to the station. Then he remembered he better sober up or he'd end up joining me in the slammer. He swore he'd be right over after a couple of hours of sobering up. Meanwhile, I was locked up, spending the remainder of Christmas Eve in a cold, dank, lonely cell.

Dr. Martin finally arrived around midnight and asked the booking sergeant if he could talk to him privately. The two of them disappeared into a small office. It was there, as Dr. Martin later told me, that he gave the sergeant a crisp hundred-dollar bill. The sergeant snapped the bill. Held it up to the light. Within a few minutes, he took a razor blade and cut out the page that showed I was booked and destroyed it.

After I was released, we were driven back to Dr. Martin's car by the police. Together, we drove back to his house. Happily, the party was still going on and all the guests we still drinking and dancing. Most importantly, I was able to entertain Mary Ann with the story of my Christmas Eve adventure.

28. Necessity is the Mother of Invention

It had been raining very hard for the past two days in Philadelphia. Sunday came, and my good friend Nathan and I decided it would be the perfect time to visit his cousins Nina and Sarah Wolf. Did I mention the girls' parents were in Florida for their winter vacation? The Wolf parents spent every winter in Florida. Conveniently, this left their girls home alone except for the housekeeper.

We drove over to their home in my "new" 1933 black Ford. It was my first car, and I'd just bought it. I was proud because I'd paid for it with my own money. It was used and about twelve years old. It did, however, have one major flaw. The right-front door was broken and wouldn't open. Of course, I didn't discover this fact until I had already paid for it and had brought it home. But it was cheap and got me around, and I've got to admit I think I had a thing for black 1930s Fords since my father had driven one.

Shortly after we arrived, the four of us started a game of pinochle to pass the time. After about an hour, we all became a little bored. Nathan, always a big eater, complained of being hungry and wanted a hoagie and a large coke. Sounded really good to all of us. We all agreed to take a break and decided to go to Pat's King of Steaks in Fairmont Park. We piled into my 1933 black Ford, ready to roll.

We were excited and ready to roll. I put my key into the ignition, put my foot on the accelerator, and turned the key. *Grau, grau, grau, grau.* The damn car wouldn't start. It was out of gas. I guess I hadn't checked if all the gauges worked on the Ford, either. You see, in those days, most gasoline stations were closed on Sundays. How and where were we going to get some gas?

Nina mentioned that her father's Cadillac was parked in the garage and that she was sure its tank was full. We opened the garage and inspected the gas tank. It was full. Now, how was I going to transfer some of that gas into my car?

I remembered my science class lesson on siphoning fluids from one container to another. I would need a long tube, but we couldn't find one in their garage. Then, with a blush, Sarah suggested that we use the tubing of her mother's douche bag, which was hanging in a bathroom over the shower door. We couldn't stop laughing, but it sounded like a great solution.

While the girls ran off to fetch the douche bag, Nathan and I pushed my Ford onto the driveway and positioned it so that its gas tank was as close as possible to the Cadillac's.

Nina and Sarah rushed back, douche bag and tubing in hand. I removed the tube from the bag and placed one end into the Cadillac's gas tank and the other end into my mouth. I had to suck out the air until the gas could begin to flow.

Sadly, I got a mouthful of gasoline in the process, which I promptly spit out. We all started to laugh and couldn't stop. I was spitting and laughing. Having placed the tube into the Ford's tank, I let the gas flow, still spitting and now howling in laughter. In the end, we must have siphoned out over half a tank of the old man's gas.

After cleaning up any mess we'd made and putting everything away in its proper place, the four of us climbed back into the old black Ford. This time, it started.

Off we drove to Pat's. By this time, Nathan wasn't the only one who was starving. I forgot about any taste of the gasoline after my second bite into my Philly cheesesteak. I wondered, as I was finally eating, if Mrs. Wolf would notice any of the gasoline missing.

29. Music, Music, Music

Our whole family was musical. My mother's brothers and sisters all played the harmonica. They were experts in playing all sorts of instruments.

My mother wanted my brother Lenny to learn how to play the piano. Dad purchased a Steinway, but Lenny showed no interest in learning. Years later, I discovered that Dad's brother Harry, who was an adagio dancer on the vaudeville stage, had stolen the instruments from the band—just to make music.

I, however, could play a horn ever since I could remember. I don't know who taught me. But I could blow. I began with a bugle, then an A-flat single valve horn, a coronet, and then a trumpet.

When I was ten years old, our family moved to our new place on 15th Street. Mike and I decided that we wanted to take music lessons, so my father brought home a saxophone for us. Mike refused to let me play it. He said that I spit in it too much. I told Dad that I wanted to play the trumpet, and so the next day he brought home my first trumpet.

Mom hired a music teacher, Mr. Yarnel, who was an accomplished musician. He could play all brass and reed instruments. He came to the house every Thursday after school and gave private lessons to the both of us for ten dollars an hour. That was some serious money. Mr. Yarnel was a good and patient teacher. He was both encouraging and kind. He always made you feel like you were making progress.

By the time I was twelve years old, I was good enough to join a marching band. The band was called The Yardley Marching Band and was sponsored by the Veterans of Foreign Wars in 1940. There were about one hundred and fifty musicians in it. I played in the first trumpet section. Our section practiced every Wednesday night and marched in local neighborhood parades. We wore black and white uniforms trimmed in white and black feathers.

The most important parade of the year was the New Year's Day Mummers Parade. The Mummers Parade is a yearly event that's been going on in Philadelphia since the 1800s to celebrate the New Year. In 1900, it became an official city event.

I remember marching down Broad Street from North Philadelphia through the center of the city. We passed City Hall down into South Philadelphia. It was so cold out that Mom made me wear her snuggies, her warm winter underwear, under my uniform. I was embarrassed and fought with her not to wear them. I lost the argument. Turned out that I was secretly thankful.

In the 1940s, the audiences along Broad Street in the freezing cold swelled to over two million together with thousands of costumed participants as bands, comics, fans clubs, floats, crossdressers, etc. You never saw so many mostly immigrant groups (Irish, Italians, Polish) drinking, laughing, playing, staggering on New Year's Day for miles.

The feathered floats and costumes took a year to prepare and stage, especially down Mummers Row on South Second Street in Little Italy.

Marching in the parade was a thrilling experience, and I was proud that I was good enough to participate. The parade was flamboyant and very feathered. There were string bands that played and danced to their music. There were clowns who juggled balls and joked around with the raucous crowds. There were dancing female impersonators and, of course, the brass bands.

Every participant was costumed in colorful sequins, feathers, and jewels. The crowds cheered and called out their approval to the passing units. Each unit was judged by a panel of city officials and politicians. In the year that I marched, our band was awarded first place.

My abilities as a trumpet player progressed rapidly, and Mr. Yarnel thought he could not teach me anything more. He suggested I find another teacher. At that time, the first trumpet player of the Philadelphia Symphony Orchestra, Saul Caston, was offering lessons at the Lehigh

Avenue Boys' Club for a small fee. Aspiring students had to try out to see if they were qualified. I played "The Carnival of Venice" at my tryout, and Mr. Caston loved it. He accepted me as a student. I was proud to have been chosen, and I practiced diligently for two to three hours a day.

I continued playing my trumpet into my high school years and on into college. When I was eighteen and a freshman at Temple University, I joined a dance band named Byron Goldberg and His Six Golden Nuggets.

Byron was a good jazz pianist. I played the trumpet. We had five other musicians in the band who played drums, saxophone, bass, trombone, and clarinet. We played at weddings, bar mitzvahs, proms, and other celebrations.

One evening in 1947, we were hired to play at a wedding at the Ambassador Hotel, an elegant hotel in Philadelphia. During a break, I heard a man calling to me, "Hey, kid, what are you doing this summer?"

I turned around and saw Woody Herman, the well-known Grammy-nominated leader of his own big band called The Herd.

I shyly told him that I would be working as a grocery clerk at the American Store during the day and on weekends would be playing with the band.

He said, "How would you like to play with my band this summer?"

I happily replied, "I'd love to!"

And so began a new life adventure that summer at nineteen years old.

30. On the Road with Woody

It was the summer of 1947 when I accepted the offer from Woody Herman to play in his band The Second Herd. What an honor! He was one of the greats in jazz. He was not only the head of one of the most popular "big bands" of the time but also a popular recording artist.

Woody was an outstanding musician playing alto and soprano saxophone. Some of the songs he made famous were "Laura," "At the Wood Choppers Ball," "Caldonia," and "The Golden Wedding." He had a reputation for hiring the best side-men for his band and for using their musical arrangements. Some of these side-men became well known in their own right.

That summer, we were scheduled to play at Birdland in New York City, at the Aragon Ballroom in Chicago, and at the Steel Pier in Atlantic City. I was to be paid $250 a week, and all living and travel expenses were to be paid by the band. This was the most money I had ever been paid for any kind of work.

At first, Mom said I couldn't go, but I was so excited about going on the road with the band and begged so repeatedly that she finally agreed. She was concerned that if I were to go away for the whole summer, I would lose my regular "real" job as a grocery clerk at the American Store.

I spoke to Frank Gurley, the manager, about my opportunity to play with Woody Herman. Turned out that Frank was an ardent jazz fan and was thrilled for me. He promised that when I returned, I would have my job back.

Byron Goldberg, leader of the Six Golden Nuggets, was delighted to have a musician in his band who'd played with one of the jazz greats. My job with him was guaranteed, too.

The day that school was out for summer vacation, I headed to 30th Street Station in Philly, in one hand holding a case with a trumpet and flugelhorn and in the other hand a battered suitcase containing a rented tuxedo and a pair of patent-leather shoes.

I took the train to New York City, where I met the band at a seedy hotel near Birdland. While on the train, people were curious about my instrument case and asked me what I played. I beamed, telling them that I played trumpet in Woody Herman's band.

I was nervous, at first, as to how the members of the band would treat me, but I needn't have worried because they were very kind and accepted me as an equal member of the group. The first trumpeter was another young musician who took me under his wing and taught me interesting and difficult techniques on my instrument, especially hitting high notes and playing spontaneous riffs.

Every morning, the band would get together to practice in the ballroom where we were scheduled to play that evening. It always seemed as if we were practicing in a cloudy haze because all of the band members smoked except me.

Practice usually lasted about two hours. Sometimes, members of other bands would come and sit in and play with us. I was thrilled to have met several well-known top jazz musicians during that time like Duke Ellington, Stan Getz, and Oscar Pettiford.

In the evening, the band was assembled in the ballroom at 8:00 p.m., dressed in our tuxedos. The room was softly lit with many crystal chandeliers, and red velvet drapery hanging to the floor covered the windows. Couples waited at the sides of the ballroom, chattering excitedly until the music began to play.

The first number was "Caldonia," and as they rushed to the dance floor, they sang to the music. The band would play until 11:00 p.m. We played all types of music: swing, foxtrot, jitterbug, and Latin. Occasionally, a woman would fancy one of the musicians and, with a smile, drop the key to her hotel room into his jacket pocket.

The summer passed quickly for me. Each month, we went to a new venue. I never tired of the routine. I gained much knowledge, both musically and in life experiences.

I returned not so happily to Philadelphia to begin my sophomore year at Temple University.

31. The Incident at the Jasper Street Station

It was one thirty in the morning. I had just completed a gig with Byron Goldberg and His Six Golden Nuggets at the Ambassador Hotel. The night was cold and dark, and I was tired and anxious to get home. I hurried through the nearly empty streets to the nearest El stop two blocks away. My black leather instrument case containing my trumpet and flugelhorn weighed heavily on my arm. I slowly climbed the steps to the train platform, bought my ticket and, when my train arrived, I settled in for the thirty-minute trip to Jasper Street.

When I got there, I left the train and descended into the Jasper Street station. All was still. Suddenly, in the darkness, I felt someone tapping me on the shoulder. Frightened, I turned around and came face to face with a drunk. When he spoke, I could smell stale alcohol and foul breath.

"Hey, buddy, ya got a smoke?" he said.

I brushed his arm away. "I don't smoke."

Without warning, he stuck his dirty hand into my jacket pocket, tearing it open, searching for a cigarette. "Yer lyin,'" he said. "I see yer a musician, and they all smoke."

Dropping my case, I took a step back so I could take a good swing at him. "Not this one," I shouted as I smacked him in the nose with my clenched fist.

Blood spurted onto his rumpled suit like water from a broken faucet. He stepped close to me, putting his face next to mine, and spit a mouthful of blood and saliva directly at me.

Infuriated, I grabbed the man by the hair and smacked his head against the brick wall. I wanted to get rid of him once and for all. He crumpled to the ground, barely conscious.

In the distance, I heard the wailing of police sirens. The station attendant, seeing the rumble down below, had called the police. The sirens stopped. Two officers stepped out of the squad car. "What's going on here?" one of them asked me

I explained to the officer what had happened. After questioning me a little more, he took my name and phone number and said they would call if more information was needed.

The drunk, still lying on the ground, began to moan loudly. The two policemen lifted him up and loaded him into the back seat of the squad car. "Let's get this guy to the hospital," one of them said.

As I heard the sound of the sirens recede, still covered with spit and blood, I started to walk the two blocks to my home.

32. The Last Bus Home

In the northwestern part of Philly is a very hilly section called Manayunk, a working-class, Catholic area. When I was growing up, there were five large Catholic churches there with schools. Three catered to the Irish, one to the Germans, and one to the Italians. When I was a junior in college, I dated a very pretty redhead from the area named Peggy Clark. She lived at the top of Green Lane, which was a very, very steep hill.

Peggy and I dated almost every Saturday night for about two years. After our date, usually to a movie and out for a snack or to a dance held at a local church, I would walk Peggy back home and stay with her until exactly 1:15 a.m. The last bus to my house left from Green Lane and Ridge Avenue at 1:30 a.m. sharp. From the bus, I would have to transfer to the Number 10 trolley to Oak Lane. If I missed it, I would have to hitchhike the fifteen miles back to my house. At this time of night, that could be dangerous.

One night, our goodbye kiss lasted a little too long, and as the hands of my watch pointed to 1:20 a.m., I grabbed my jacket and raced out the door. Down Green Lane I sped, racing to make up the five minutes that I had so delightfully lost.

Suddenly, I heard a gruff voice call out in the night, "Get that guy! There he goes!"

I looked around and saw two uniformed Philadelphia cops with guns drawn. Turns out they were in hot pursuit of a burglar who'd just attempted a break-in at one of the neighborhood homes. I must have looked very suspicious to them tearing down the hill at one in the morning.

I feared for my life as I saw the pistols waving in the air.

"Stop! Stop!" yelled the officers.

I didn't want to stop. I didn't want to miss my bus, and I feared being shot no matter what the policemen said. So I ran even faster, my legs aching and my lungs gasping for air. As I reached the bottom of Green Lane, I could see my bus pulling up to a stop at Ridge Avenue. I dashed across the street against a red light and jumped into the bus just as the doors closed and it sped away. The driver was unaware that he had been my savior.

It was two o'clock in the morning when I opened the door to my house, my usual coming home time on the weekend.

My mother called out, "Are you okay, Bern?"

"Yeah, Mom, I'm okay. Go to sleep. Forget about it."

33. My College Prom

"Mrs. Greenberg, may I please borrow your car for next Saturday night?" I asked. "I need transportation to get to my senior prom."

"I'll have to ask Jack," she said with a smile, referring to her husband. "By the way, how long have you been driving?"

"I got my license a year ago, and have never had an accident," I replied.

"I'll let you know by tomorrow," said Mrs. Greenberg.

It was 1950, the end of my senior year at Temple University in North Philadelphia. I was heading toward graduation with honors, with a major in chemistry, and I was looking forward to the ceremonies and festivities that would accompany the commencement.

I was especially excited about my senior prom. It would be held in the ballroom of Minton Hall, a beautiful stone Gothic building on campus. Tony Pastor and his orchestra, which was one of the most popular big bands of the day, would be playing.

I had invited Peggy Clark to be my date. She was a terrific dancer. She was looking forward to the prom as much as I was, but I had one problem—no transportation! And so I began my desperate search to find some.

The following morning, Mrs. Greenberg, our neighbor, gave me the disappointing news that her husband thought me much too young to trust with the family's Chrysler. I had asked other neighbors, too, but they'd also turned me down.

I was having lunch with my friend Bob Boyer at Temple's cafeteria that noon. I asked him if he was planning to go to the prom. He was. I pushed him on my woes concerning transportation. Amazing, pay dirt finally: he had transportation. I asked if he could make room for another couple.

"Plenty of room," he said.

I was ecstatic. At last, my problem was solved.

The night of the prom came. I put on my black rented tuxedo and my starched white shirt. I had bought a double orchid corsage for sweet Peggy. Right on time, I heard the loud honking of a horn. My ride had arrived. I opened the front door and my jaw dropped.

Parked in front was a long, black, shiny hearse. Bob, beaming his dumb grin, called out for me to "come on down." As I got in, I saw the whole back end of the hearse, which was where the coffin usually went, was filled with white lilies and red roses. Swinging around and throwing my arm over his shoulder in friendship, I gave him a knowing squeeze.

"Where the hell did you get a hearse?"

"My brother's a mortician," he answered. "Yeah, we had a funeral this morning, so I kept the flowers. Nice touch, don't you think?"

I shrugged, knowing I had to agree. As Bob, his date, and I drove to pick up Peggy, I was getting more than a little worried as to what her reaction might be. She was going to the prom in a hearse and didn't know it. But not to worry or fret. She was delighted when she saw the shiny black vehicle.

"What fun!" she said.

We had a great time that evening. During an intermission, I went up and asked Tony Pastor if the band was going to play the popular song "Peg O' My Heart." He replied that it was. People expected it.

Never known for my subtlety or modesty, I brought him up to speed about my time with Woody Herman and the trumpet. That was when I asked if he would let me play the trumpet solo to impress my date, Peggy. He laughed out loud and was in on it.

As soon as the intermission was over, Tony called me up on the bandstand and introduced me to my fellow classmates. The band began nice and slow, and I soloed to a jazzy rendition of "Peg O' My Heart."

The crowd cheered. More importantly, my Peg—my wild Irish rose— was delighted.

On the way home, Peggy snuggled against me in the back of the hearse.

The scent of the roses and lilies still lingered in the air.

She leaned her head on my shoulder and said, "I never thought riding in a hearse could be so much fun."

34. Ready, Willing, and Able

I graduated with honors from Temple University, majoring in chemistry. I thought that joining the US Army would be an exciting experience given I was twenty-two years old. My mother protested. Gotta remember that my older brother had been discharged from the Navy after serving in World War II, and my younger brother was attending the US naval flight mechanics' school in Atlanta, Georgia. It was a kind of family tradition, it seemed to me. So I wrote a letter, unbeknownst to Mom, to the draft board volunteering to join. Five weeks later, I received a letter asking me to report to the draft board for a physical examination prior to my induction into the Army. I reported to an old courthouse building that had been remodeled into an induction center. A doctor examined me, after which I was sent for lab tests. When being given a urinalysis bottle, many men would add substances that would taint the results and cause them to be rejected, classified 4F. I was classified 1A.

I went home and one month later received a letter informing me that I was drafted and to report to the induction center from which I would be transported by bus to Fort Dix, New Jersey. I was among the earliest draftees for this emerging conflict, together with what would be 220,000 other young men that year.

When I arrived, I was issued a uniform and equipment, and everything that I might need for basic infantry training. The next day, all of us inductees were given various intelligence and aptitude tests. The soldiers that scored high were offered an opportunity to attend OCS (Officer Candidate School), which meant they would have to stay in the Army for four years. I did well and scored high, but refused this "opportunity" because I didn't want to be committed to another two years of service.

That was when I was assigned to the Chemical Corps. After six weeks of basic infantry training, I was sent to Edgewood, Maryland. There, I was trained to monitor atom bomb tests. The unit was called the Radiological Survey Team. We learned to measure radioactive fallout after an atomic bomb had been dropped. We also experimented with G-agents. These are poison gasses for which there is no detection or antidote. They were developed by the Germans during World War II. We used beagle hounds in our experiments. They were cooperative and easy to work with.

On the post, the Army had built spectacular laboratories where all weather conditions could be simulated, (heat, cold, humidity, and wind velocity). Some of the experiments with G-agents could be quite dangerous and produce symptoms such as nausea, vomiting, headaches, and diarrhea. The Army would reward a soldier with a weekend pass if he volunteered to participate in one of these experiments. For example, a soldier would hold a canary in a birdcage within an enclosed chamber. Gas would be released. If there were any symptoms observed, the experiments would be terminated.

The big day had come. We hadn't volunteered or been trained, but we saddled up. We were going to be participants in an atomic bomb test.

Our unit was flown to Dugway Proving Ground in Utah about eighty-five miles southwest of Salt Lake City. We knew it was a testing ground out in the western Utah desert of over 26,000 square miles. Seemed like the right place for the test.

We got about our business, yet now we were introduced to some new equipment. We had been sent out here to collect the necessary equipment to do a survey of a bomb drop (dosimeters, mono-meters, and paraffin-injected clothes). Just "to keep 'em guessing." That was when we were flown off at night to Frenchman Flats in Nevada.

35. What a Bargain? In the Army...

It was a bright, sunny day at the Army Chemical Center in Edgewood, Maryland, where I was stationed for six months in 1950. The Center was located next to the Aberdeen Proving Grounds, where the Army tested its firepower with an assortment of heavy weapons. We were also next to Camp Detrick, where the Army tested its biological weapons. Because of their close proximity, the three camps shared one gigantic PX (Post Exchange).

This huge PX sold everything a modern department store or drugstore or market might carry. In addition, you could buy cars, tools, and all kinds of mechanical equipment. All of these items could be purchased at ten percent above wholesale. It was a buyer's delight. Having experienced the shortages, rationing, and restrictions just a few years earlier, this was every military family's dream come true.

On this particular day, I was making plans to go home on leave for the weekend. I went to the PX to buy some things to resell to my friends at home. Items were so cheap here that I could sell them at a discount and still make a small profit for myself. As I pushed my shopping cart up and down the aisles, I tossed in ten cartons of cigarettes at a dollar fifty a carton, ten decks of playing card at fifteen cents a deck, and two boxes of candy bars at three bars for ten cents.

Then I passed the pharmacy section. I noticed a sign advertising condoms at two cents apiece. What a bargain! I approached the clerk, a little old lady, and asked for two gross. She went to the back of the pharmacy and came back with two sheets of Silvertex condoms.

"I'm sorry," she said. "Three are missing. We have only one hundred and forty-one condoms. Do you still want them?"

"That's okay, I'll take them," I replied.

I spent my weekend leave back at home happily and profitably. I spent time with family and friends, went to a few parties, and sold all of the merchandise. My friends even placed orders for more on my next leave home.

My friends drove me to 30th Street Station, where I caught the last train from Philadelphia back to Edgewood. The train was loaded with servicemen and there were no seats available, so I had to stand for the three-hour train ride. It was hot and stuffy. I took off my overcoat and tossed it onto the overhead rack and fell asleep, standing up for the whole ride back to camp.

"Edgewood, Edgewood," the conductor called out as we pulled into the station at six o'clock in the morning.

I grabbed an overcoat from the overhead rack and hopped off the train. I proceeded to camp to stand reveille in an overcoat that was three sizes too small. The sergeant called me out and handed me a slip to go to the quartermaster to get a coat that fit.

A few days later, I had some spare time, so I returned to the PX to look around. As I neared the pharmacy, the little old lady who had sold me the condoms approached me. She was followed by an entourage of women clerks, all smiling and giggling.

"Well, soldier," she said, smiling. "It's good to see you again. I hope we didn't spoil your weekend."

36. An Autumn Adventure

Every autumn, the eastern states are a profusion of colors. From the red, orange, and yellow leaves ready to fall from the deciduous trees, to the dark-green needles of the conifers, to the sparkling waters of the rivers, streams, and lakes, the landscape there is like an artist's palate. In 1950, I was pretty much stationed full-time amid this beautiful countryside.

Nina Wolf, my current flame, was a cute, seventeen-year-old brunette. She was a cousin of one of my best friends, Nathan Wolf, and was a senior in high school. One weekend, because I was unable to get a pass to go to Philadelphia, Nina decided to drive to Edgewood to visit me. This came as a complete surprise to me.

I was walking around the camp doing nothing in particular when I heard the loudspeaker blare my name. "Private Bernard Cohen, report to headquarters."

My heart was stuck in my throat as I reviewed every stupid thing I'd said and done over the last twenty-four hours, then last week. I knew I was one cooked goose. When I arrived at post headquarters, I was astonished, delighted, and beyond relieved to see Nina standing there.

I escorted her proudly to the mess hall. It was lunchtime, and what better way to introduce her to fine dining, Army-style. The guys fell backward, eyes popping open wide. My buddies apparently approved of Nina. She was "hot stuff."

After lunch, we explored the post. I showed her the small museum at the company headquarters that displayed the equipment of the Chemical Corps and items related to its history.

We spent the rest of the day exploring and walking through the lovely countryside. Believe it or not, we dined a second time at chow. You see, time flew when we were with each other. It was getting real late, and we had gotten so caught up in time.

I thought it would be dangerous for her to drive the two-and-a-half hours back to Philadelphia in the dark. Now I had to try to find accommodations for the night for her. Of course by now, all visitor accommodations at the post were occupied. I called the few nearby motels and there, too, all rooms were taken. So much for careful planning.

That was when I remembered the church. It was drenched in light during the day and dark as could be at night. You see, there was a large non-denominational church on base. It was open twenty-four hours. Also, it was heated and safe. This was where we would sleep.

We snuck back to my barracks and picked up some blankets and pillows, returned to the church, and settled down for the night.

In the meantime, back in Philly, Nina's older sister returned home from a date. Not finding her little sister safely in bed, she became hysterical. These were the parents who were always vacationing in Florida for the winter. The sister called everyone who might know of Nina's whereabouts. She even rang my brother Mike, waking him from a sound sleep.

"How the hell should I know where your sister is?" a very sleepy and angry Mike replied.

In the morning, after reveille, we wisely had breakfast together at a restaurant off-post. We nervously kissed goodbye and laughed about our adventure together. I returned to camp rather ruffled and exhausted.

Nina's sister never spoke to me again. On the other hand, neither of us got in trouble with either her parents, my mother, or the US military industrial complex.

Thanks, sis. I still owe you.

37. The Big Boom

The atomic bomb is different from conventional bombs. Bombs destroy property, and based on their target strike will also kill a certain number of combatants and civilians. Atomic bombs not only destroy property, but they obliterate all life in the measurable area instantaneously through the fireball and over time by producing deadly radiation.

As you remember, in the spring of 1951, I was flown to Dugway Proving Ground in Utah as part of a survey team to measure the radiological fallout from an atomic blast. At that early stage of nuclear inquiry, we were equipped with paraffin-impregnated clothing and shoes as well as instruments such as dosimeters, manometers, and ion chambers used to measure radiation fallout. Apparently, we were to become human guinea pigs!

Years later, it became clear Dugway was not the right site for the continued atmospheric test explosions given the proximity of Salt Lake City. So the following morning, we were flown to Alamogordo for the atomic test itself.

The bomb was suspended on a reinforced stainless steel tower approximately thirty feet high and was surrounded by scientific equipment that was remotely controlled. About ten thousand feet away were bunkers. These bunkers were made of stainless steel and buried in the ground. There were reinforced slit-like glass windows. Twenty soldiers occupied each bunker. Less fortunate, but certainly also unaware, were whole companies of soldiers out in the open used as "observers."

A warning bell rang, which meant that the bomb would be detonated in three minutes. *BOOMMMM!* We were instructed to open our mouths to reduce the potential percussive destruction to the brain from the explosive wave. The explosion came as an intense light that illuminated the mountains ten miles away. Then there was a sudden wave of heat, and later a tremendous roar as a shock wave passed and echoed through the valley. A ball of fire rose rapidly, followed by a mushroom cloud extending to approximately forty thousand feet in the sky.

The tower had been completely vaporized, and the desert sand surrounding it had been fused into glass for eight hundred yards around its base. The explosion we observed was the equivalent to twenty-thousand tons of TNT. I was amazed at the massive destruction and shuddered to think of the devastation that would occur not only to our country but to the rest of the world if there were an atomic war.

After two hours when the dust and dirt had settled, we opened the door of the bunker and began our survey. As we walked back and forth measuring the radiation, we looked like men walking on a moonscape. Nothing was alive.

Two days later, when the survey had been completed, we were flown by seaplane (no other planes were available) to Anacostia, a naval airbase in Washington, DC, where we landed on the river. When we arrived at the Army Chemical Center in Maryland, I was told to report to Headquarters Company. The commanding officer told me that I was being transferred to the 187th Regimental Combat Team.

I asked, "Why am I being transferred?"

He replied that I could not get top security clearance because of my father's criminal activities and that he had never become a citizen of the United States.

I was still Whitey's son—now with collateral damage.

38. The Transfer

I arrived in Fort Benning, Georgia, in the dead of night. I was assigned to the 187th Regimental Combat Team.

"Welcome," said the sergeant. "We train the "fightingest" parachute soldiers in the Army. It's not going to be easy. I'll see you at six o'clock in the morning."

We woke to the sound of a bugle blowing reveille and were dressed and out within ten or fifteen minutes. After breakfast, we were sent to a class instructing us on the care of parachutes. We learned how to put them on, how to fold them, and how to repack them after we jumped. We learned how to hide them, if needed, after landing so we would not be discovered. We learned how to fire mortars and machine guns and how to escape from trees or rooftops. The training was intense.

Finally, at the end of six weeks, I was ready for my first jump. The plane flew over a wooded area near the base. A green light flashed, a buzzer sounded, and the jump sergeant yelled, "Let's go! Stand up! Latch on! Move out!"

One by one, we soldiers jumped out of the plane.

When I jumped, I pulled the rip cord but my chute didn't open. I was sure I was going to die. I gathered my wits about me and pulled the cord on the emergency chute. *Bang!* It flew gloriously open. I glided safely to the ground and landed on my feet. *Hurrah.*

After ten safe jumps, I graduated from jump school. We were all given an aptitude test to determine our strengths, and as I scored high in science, so it was decided that I should become a paramedic. I was then transferred to Fort Sam Houston in Texas for training to become a paramedic.

The training was excellent. In the six weeks I was at Fort Sam Houston,

I learned how to take care of injured and sick soldiers. We were taught by board-certified emergency room physicians.

I really enjoyed my time there. It was a life-changing experience that raised my possible horizons.

I was given a two-week furlough to go home and then was transferred to Fort Lawton in Seattle, Washington. From there, we shipped out to Camp Drake (a joint Army and Air Force base) in Asoka, Japan, after which we would be sent to Korea to join our unit, the 187th.

39. On My Way to War

"Private Bernard Cohen 52 036 468 reporting for duty, Sir!" I said.

"You're assigned to barrack number 14, bed 24," the officer of the day responded sharply. "Further information will be posted on the bulletin board in your barracks."

The date was November 1, 1951, when I arrived at Fort Lawton, overlooking Puget Sound in Seattle. Fort Lawton was the second-largest replacement and deployment centers for soldiers going to Korea. Over one million US soldiers passed through there during WWII. Now it was our turn.

The post was shabby and in need of repair. The barracks were old and dilapidated, having been used so heavily during World War II. The only heat in each barrack came from two small wood-burning stoves, not nearly enough for the size of the building nor the cold damp weather of a Seattle winter. In fact, during my stay of a week, some of the soldiers would strip the wood from the barrack walls to feed the fire. There was never enough fuel provided.

During my stay in Fort Lawton, I, along with other soldiers, was oriented with the customs, manners, and basic language of the Korean people. We were shown films and heard lectures on the rules of engagement in battle. Our evenings were free, however, and we could enjoy the sights and pleasures of Seattle in any way we pleased.

On the 8th of November, three hundred soldiers were transported by bus to Bremerton, Washington, also on the Puget Sound, where the Navy had an established base. From there, we were to be shipped by the Navy-Army Transport Service (NATS) to Japan. As we tramped up the gangway of the Kaiser Liberty Ship, the Sergeant Allan Edwards, we were accompanied by an Army marching band playing "Over There." The patriotic music stirred my spirits.

The sailing was smooth at the outset of our two-week voyage to Japan. As we passed through the Sound, we watched a new Fred Astaire movie on the deck of the ship. However, when we entered the open waters of the Pacific, a wild storm whipped up with torrents of rain and heaving waves.

The storm lasted for the better part of a week while the ship rolled and pitched. The bow would pitch high into the air and then come crashing down into the sea, causing the whole ship to tremble and shake.

We troops were confined below. For our safety, it was a court-martialing offense to venture onto the deck. Most of us were seasick and vomiting into the head. When the ship heaved, the vomitus and excrement would splash onto any unfortunate who was too close.

One soldier who wanted fresh air disregarded orders and went on deck. He was never seen again. He was washed overboard by the raging waves. We tried the best we could to sleep in hammocks with our weapons tucked in beside us. This storm lasted a miserable five days and nights.

The storm finally abated. During the remaining days of our journey, the sea began to calm. We finally arrived at Yokohama in Tokyo Bay at ten in the morning, scheduled to disembark at noon. The Navy got crews in to clean up the mess in the head. Then they locked the latrines at ten o'clock. They didn't have to clean again for the return voyage. So no toilets were available to us, the impatient and waiting troops. Many of the men were still sick and had diarrhea resulting from the evening meal. They were forced to use their helmets as a toilet and throw the waste overboard. The ship stank. We soldiers stank even more when we finally disembarked at noon. There was no welcoming music as we boarded the waiting buses to take us to Camp Drake in Asoka, Japan.

Camp Drake was surrounded by cornfields. Soldiers in transit to Korea were not permitted to leave camp. In the evenings, after a day of lectures, we would be prodded with a stick to keep us awake. When we weren't being prepared for battle, we were bored with nothing to do.

It was at that time that "Ping Pong Boys" would pop up like magic in the middle of the cornfields, yelling, "Hey, G.I., I got a girl for you. Ten dollars for your pleasure." This was how it worked. An interested soldier would follow the "Ping Pong Boy" through the cornfields to one of many whorehouses. At the other end of the field, these women were beautiful and obliging. There were many of them. Before entering a house, as is custom in Japan, you had to take off your shoes and leave them neatly at the doorway.

It was easy to identify a soldier who had broken the rules. The post's MPs would go to the houses and collect the boots and bring them back to the MP station at the camp's gate. A shoeless soldier returning to camp needed to pick up his boots. The soldier would be warned but not punished, and he would be driven back to his barrack. Korea would be punishment enough.

Now the jig was really up. Very soon, way too soon, I was on my way to war.

40. The Real Deal: First Drop into Battle

We were all nervous about the prospect of going into battle. Some soldiers had been in combat and returned to camp tense and edgy.

I recall one soldier who was sitting on a blanket on the ground next to a group of men playing cards. Disposing of a cigarette butt, he flipped it toward a butt can. It missed and landed on the blanket where the men were playing. He apologized, but one of the card players stood up, grabbed a rifle, and hit him in the jaw, breaking it and knocking out most of the soldier's teeth. I dared to accompany the injured soldier to the first-aid station and was happy that I hadn't been hit in the jaw, too.

In a few days, our unit was fully mustered and combat ready. This was our unit's first operation in Korea. We were airborne and heading for North Korea, where we were supposed make our jump. But by tragic error, we were dropped on the Chinese side of the Yalu River.

There were thousands of Chinese soldiers below. They looked like ants on the ground as I parachuted down. They were everywhere. The sound of battle bugles blowing rose up to meet us. The rhythmic beating battle drums came closer as we descended faster. And then they were firing everything at us.

By pure luck, I landed safely and made it into a depression in the ground. It was a crater of a spent artillery shell hit.

This was the beginning of my good luck. Then the shooting began for us. And that was when the tough luck for everyone around me unfolded.

Clockwise (from top left): Sadie and Herman "Whitey" Cohen, parents of Bernard Louis Koire. Lenny, Bernie, and Mike Koire with an unidentified friend. Bernie as a medic in Korea.

Top: Mike, Bernie, and Lenny Koire begin new life in Los Angeles.
Bottom: Bernie meets Nina Rose Levy at the University of Southern California.

Top: Bernie and Nina at wedding (1954).
Bottom: Sadie and her three sons at Bernie and Nina's wedding.

Top: The Koire Family: Dr. and Mrs. Bernard Koire along with their daughters, Alison and Hillary. This was at Alison's Bat Mitzvah at Wilshire Boulevard Temple with Rabbi Edgar F Magnin (1968). Bottom: Teenagers Hillary and Alison with Bernie.

Bernie on a donkey in Santorini, Greece.

Iquitos April 6, 1971

Mr.
Bernard Koire
Suite 1107
9255 Sunset Boulevard
L
Dear Mr. Bernard Koire:

Today we are much obliged to God, because, we may write once again and desire our Everlasting Father's richest blessings.

In our Peruvian Orient Mission, ex-Amazon Mission Thirty-five indian languages are spoken; their cultures and customs are very interesting and Christianism h made its incredible miracles. Strong point of Evangelism is to Educate, but a rious problem is the lack of some boarding-Academy School Students to teach th pupils who are finishing Elementary School. We certainly believe that you hav received our Christmas Card, showing the work we realize in this Mission.

We have wonderful brother here, but, they are not able to help us, as they wou like due the major part are indian people. They are poor and most of them liv on mountains and valleys, and in: Amazon, Ucayali, Tigres and Marañón river ba Please pray for the work in this Mission, Stahl Clinic, Ucayali Academy and El mentary Schools.

As we have a monthly slip of paper, everyday in our worship morning we pray fo one of our missionaries, brothers and friends there in the United States, and brothers' birthday. We are praying for you on April 30th.

We are very anxious to invite you to keep a walken just here in order to get i touch with this curious and beautiful nature, so you rest a moment from the sm asphalt and congestioned transit from your dear and beauty country.

OH! By the Lord's Grace our planes are flying again after been grounded almost year. Soon, we are starting the work with the new launch together with Clyde Peters' aeroplane and the radio.

Awaiting for your welcome and soon reply to our letter, we pray to God asking Him to bless you and grant you a good health, and wisdom in your work.

With brotherly love,

Itamar Sabino de Paiva
President

ISP/ hbb

TELEGRAMAS
"ADVENTISTAS"   CASILLA 240
                        IQUITOS PERU   CORONEL PORTIL
                                              TELÉFONOS 2290

Letter inviting Bernie on a mission to Peru.

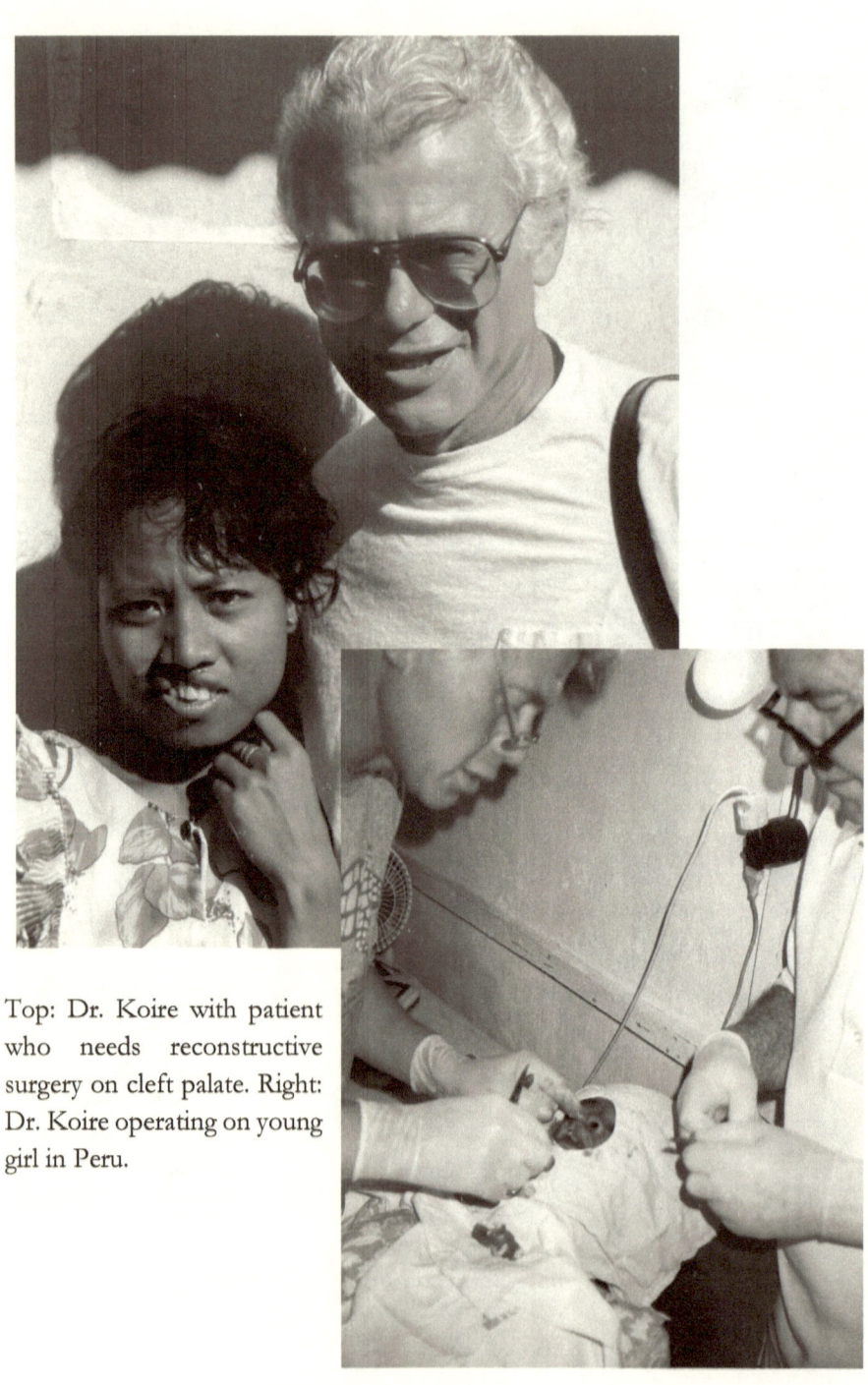

Top: Dr. Koire with patient who needs reconstructive surgery on cleft palate. Right: Dr. Koire operating on young girl in Peru.

Top: Nina and Bernie at the Taj Mahal, one of their many adventures. Bottom: Nina in New Guinea, which was a place that Bernie and she traveled to on multiple medical missions.

Top: Bernie in Africa holding a lion cub. Bottom: Bernie on a family trip to Egypt.

Top: Bernie and Nina on anniversary cruise to Alaska. Bottom: Bernie
photographed with a snake in Morocco.

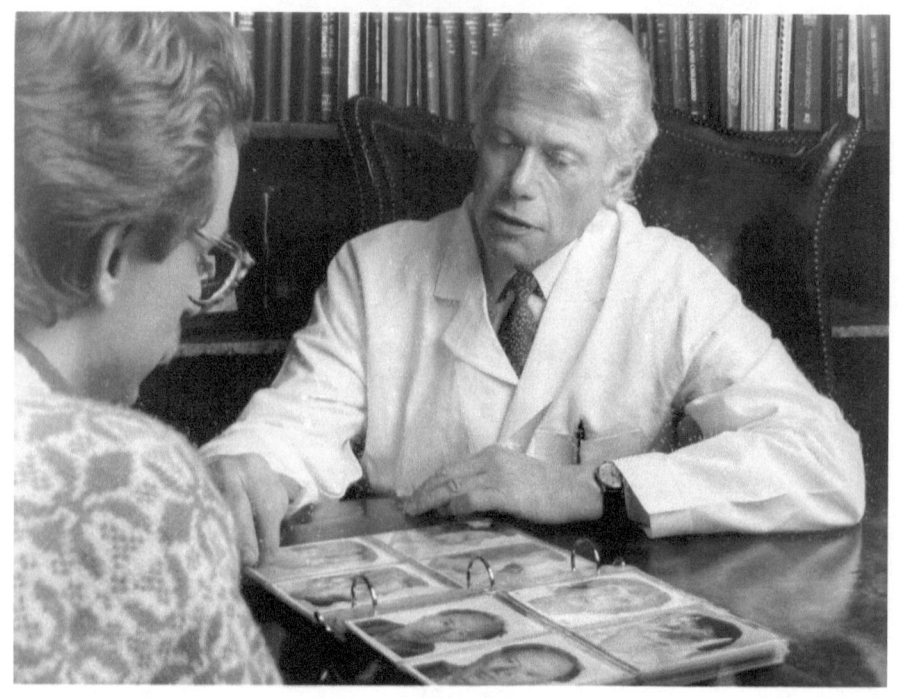

Dr. Bernard Koire during a consultation with a patient at his office on
Sunset Boulevard in Beverly Hills.

41. The Lost Bet that Saved My Life

"We need whole blood and plasma," the sergeant said. "Bernie and Joe, go to the station hospital and pick 'em up, pronto."

The 187th—the "Rakkasans"—was decimated by our jump. By some lousy error of the air command, we were dropped behind enemy lines in China. A combined force of five thousand men made that jump, and half of them were lost, killed by enemy fire. This fiasco is still being debated and studied.

I was a medic in the 187th, as was my buddy, Joe Shaw. We were in a forward aid station situated on the battlefield where the wounded were first brought. There were so many wounded that we quickly ran short of our supply of blood and plasma.

In civilian life, Joe was a car mechanic, and probably a damn good one. He was quite a bit older than me. You see, he was a WWII vet. After his discharge, he joined the Army Reserve and was called back in when the Korean War broke out. As a very experienced paratrooper, Joe was now assigned as a medic to the 187th. I looked up to Joe.

Winters in Korea are severe. It was the winter of 1951. It was freezing cold, and the sleet came down in torrents, sounding like bullets as it hit our helmets. The sky was gray and overcast but slashed with streaks of red from the enemy's artillery fire and mortars. The ground was muddy and slippery. There were no paved roads, only compressed tracks made by passing tank units.

Joe and I were exhausted from carrying the wounded from the disastrous battlefield, so neither of us wanted to drive. We decided to flip a coin. Heads was the winner and could be the passenger and try to get some shut-eye. Tails was the loser and had to drive. We flipped the coin, each holding our breath. I lost.

The only available vehicle was an ambulance, which we G.I.s called "a cracker box." It would be a twenty-mile drive through hell to get to the station hospital to pick up the blood and plasma.

Off we went over the rough tank tracks, crossing the Yalu River on a tattered and teetering pontoon bridge. We continued driving at a breakneck speed while dodging the potholed terrain, mortars and artillery firing overhead. Finally, we reached the station hospital. The hospital had been radioed that we were coming, and the needed supply was quickly loaded into the cracker box.

We wanted to get back to the front before dark, knowing that with the headlights on, we would be sitting ducks. The artillery was even more intense on the way back. Nervously, we were yapping. Joe and I were talking about our families back home when an artillery shell crashed through the window of the ambulance. I lost control of the vehicle and crashed into a deep crater that had been left by a falling bomb.

I looked to my right. There was Joe. He was dead. His head was half detached from his body, hanging on only by the bones of his spine. I was scared and in shock. This nice guy, this family man—my buddy was gone. Why him and not me?

By chance, a truck passed by and the driver, seeing this messy situation, offered to help. He attached a chain from his truck to the front end of the cracker box. He pulled me right out of the crater. He had done this before stateside.

By some miracle, the engine choked to a start. With poor Joe still in the passenger seat, I covered him with a tarp. I delivered the needed blood and plasma back to the forward aid station as quickly as possible. After that, I respectfully took Joe's body to his temporary resting place. Dead soldiers were collected and stored at "the grave registration company." It was a quiet, lonely ending, however still in the company of your fellow soldiers.

From time to time, I still think of Joe. I wonder about that miracle. By chance, I lost that bet, the toss of a coin that placed me in the driver's seat instead of Joe.

42. The Death of Charlie Shanks

The next day, I was sent out with another medic, Charlie Shanks. Charlie was from Tennessee and had been a pig farmer. But Charlie had decided that he wanted to make the Army his career.

Charlie had joined at the end of WWII. When the Korean War broke out about six years later, he was assigned to the Airborne187th Regimental Combat Team. That was how we met during medic training. I had come to know Charlie and liked him a lot.

Charlie was a pleasant guy, a heavy smoker, who was always talking about his hunting dogs. It seemed to me that he missed his dogs more than his wife. He spoke with a heavy Southern drawl that I used to tease him about as he teased me about my Philadelphia accent. Charlie had wiry blond hair, wore glasses, and was tall and lanky, but he was strong from his years of heavy labor as a farmer and his service in the Army.

We wandered about the farmland that was now a deserted battlefield, looking for the wounded. It was freezing, nineteen degrees below zero, and the snow on the ground had hardened. We saw no wounded soldiers who were still alive. We tagged the frozen bodies of the dead we found. We readied their bodies for grave registration, a squad that would come by later to pick up the corpses for burial.

As we tramped through the crunching snow, I saw a farmhouse in the distance. I called to Charlie to join me in search of any wounded that might be hiding in that war-torn structure.

As we approached, we heard no sounds but the oinking and snorting of pigs. We found a large enclosure a short distance away from the farmhouse filled with a herd of hogs. Most of the hogs and sows were huge, but interspersed were a few piglets scampering around.

Charlie looked over the enclosure and said, smiling, "We're going to have roast pig for dinner tonight."

With his gun cocked, he opened the gate and walked into the enclosure that was muddy and slippery from the melted snow. He closed the gate behind him. A huge sow, seemingly enraged by his intrusion, rushed Charlie and knocked him down. He lay on his back in the mud, helpless, his gun knocked out of his hand.

The sow, who apparently had not been fed in some time, took a bite out of his face. I was watching this absurd scene unfold. Charlie screamed, and I began to shoot the sow with my M-1 rifle from outside the pen.

This didn't make any difference to the other hogs, who began to attack Charlie. It was a frenzied attack of biting and eating. I emptied my M-1 rifle into the herd and then went on to my 45-caliber revolver, but Charlie's cries for help stopped. I continued to kill many of the hogs. But this did not deter the rest.

Within a horrifying fifteen minutes, the attack was finished. Charlie was gone. I was at a loss, and stunned by his death. There wasn't much left of him but his glasses, boots, scraps of clothes, and bits of bone.

I felt guilty that I couldn't help him more. Given the ongoing frenzy of the pigs, I was afraid to go into the pen, but I was eventually able to reach through the fence to retrieve one of his dog tags and his glasses. The other tag I left for the grave registration.

When I returned to the forward aid station with all I could retrieve from Charlie's body, I rattled off what had happened. Nobody could believe me. It was too horrible a death. I didn't care what they said. I had seen it.

Charlie Shanks' death was recorded by the Army as "killed in action."

43. A Wounded Soldier

"Medic!"

I heard a hoarse whisper of a cry from the other side of my crater and my shelter. "I'm coming!" I yelled back over the sounds of battle.

I was loaded down with military and medical equipment. We were getting torn up. Shells were whistling through the air. There was a tremendous explosion when a shell hit a metal or concrete object. There was a fetid, toxic odor over the battleground. I snaked across the battlefield and climbed into an eight-by-ten-foot foxhole. A heavyset Black soldier was huddled against the dirt wall, crying, "Help me!"

I examined him but couldn't find any wounds. With tears in his eyes, he cried, "My belly hurts." There was a profuse bloody discharge from both his nose and his mouth. I thought he might have a ruptured liver or spleen from the concussions of the exploding shells. I knew that he would have to be flown to Tokyo General Hospital.

All at once, I felt a throbbing pain in my own upper-left thigh. There was a large, gaping wound. The bleeding was profuse. Now working on automatic, I applied a tourniquet to my leg to control the bleeding.

I got a strong adrenal rush and, with a surge of strength, heaved the wounded soldier up onto my shoulder and carried him over the battlefield through a barrage of bullets and mortar fire until I reached the forward aid station. When I put him down on a cot, he was dead. I'm sure I contributed to his death by disturbing his internal wounds.

I could feel my heart beating in my mouth. I was confused by the artillery bursting around me and the soldiers crying desperately for help. My vision was gone because of the heavy dust in the atmosphere.

I thought, *I almost got killed carrying a dead man.*

My hands were shaking, and I was exhausted. I pulled a large piece of shrapnel out of my thigh. I could see my femoral artery beating strongly. I thought, *Please, God, don't take my leg.* That's the last thing I remember.

I was flown from the rear aid station in Korea by hospital plane to a hospital in Tokyo, where doctors removed the remaining shrapnel. I remained in hospital recuperating for six weeks.

When I returned to Korea, I was honored by a large parade at Pusan Headquarters. I was awarded the Silver Star for bravery and the Purple Heart. It was presented to me by the base commander, General Matthew Ridgeway.

I was reassigned to the 8th Army 12th General Dispensary. We were five thousand men, half of whom would die in this operation. Many of the more brave and seasoned men had previously served with the 187th in World War II.

In the Army, they say, "A wounded soldier is a better soldier."

44. The Twelfth General Dispensary

After my wounds were treated and healed at Tokyo General Hospital, I was transferred back to Pusan, Korea, and the 12th General Dispensary of the 8th Army. The dispensary was located in several contiguous buildings that the Army had taken over in the harbor area. Our unit of ten technicians in the dispensary was headed by a young officer, Captain Bephler, who had been in the ROTC at Ohio State University. Under him was Lieutenant Cox, who was in charge of the lab. He was a burned-out veteran of World War II. Cox was also a chronic alcoholic and walked around the lab drunk most of the time.

I was assigned to do microscopic examinations of the body fluids of soldiers going to Japan for rest and relaxation. This was to check for venereal diseases. If a soldier had a disease, his R&R (rest and recuperation) would be denied. He would be treated at the dispensary and then be sent back to his unit on the front line for another three months. It was the Army approach toward deterrence.

Every day, we tested twenty to seventy soldiers for venereal diseases and general health. All were anxious to get this examination over with so that they could proceed by ship to Japan for R&R. On one particularly busy day, I remember a sergeant yelling at me, "Hey, Cohen, you Jew bastard, let's get this show on the road!" Then he continued, "You Jews don't know what combat is like."

His insults and taunts made my blood boil. With my history of battles, combat injuries, and decorations for bravery, I couldn't let these insults go unpunished. I marked his slide as positive for gonorrhea, even though it showed no signs of the disease. The sergeant protested that he hadn't been near a woman for six months. So I took the slide over to my buddy, who had overheard the whole conversation, insults and all. Knowingly, he carefully examined the slide. Pursing his lips, he shook his head and confirmed my diagnosis. "Yep, you've got lots of gonorrhea," he told the furious sergeant.

Then there was Willy Mitchell, who had been a friend and neighbor when I lived on 15th Street in Philadelphia. Now, of all things, he was a regular patient of mine at the 12th General Dispensary. As a teenager, he was skinny and homely with kinky hair and glasses. He wasn't particularly smart, either. He never dated when I knew him back then. In Korea, Willy seemed focused on making up for lost time.

Almost every week, he came to the clinic to be tested for gonorrhea, and almost every week, he tested positive and was treated. When I asked him why he didn't wear a condom, he replied that he hated them and that they weren't "natural" enough for him.

I tried to convince him, warning of the possibility of some more serious, chronic disease. (Did I mention Willy was not that bright?) But to no avail, he persisted in this self-destructive, risky behavior. Willy must have been transferred out or maybe even killed on the front line. I never saw him again.

Lieutenant Cox was our lab officer. He was not only an alcoholic but a sadistic drunk. For example, while doing a biopsy of lesions of the penis, he chose to forgo the use of local anesthetic. I could hear soldiers yell and scream in pain when he was doing a procedure. He seemed to rejoice in a patient's pain, saying that they deserved it. No one in our unit had any respect for him or liked him.

On the lighter side, there was a lot of camaraderie in our unit. We were a happy group, caring for one another and trying to solve one another's problems. Even with this war that occupied our every minute and surrounded us, we could laugh and even play tricks on each other. Pranks were our specialty—like short-sheeting beds or putting frogs in shoes or nailing shoes to the floor.

In the evenings, we would often play cards. Frequently, our conversations drifted to our plans for civilian life after we were discharged.

At this point, I wasn't sure about my future plans. What I did know was that I would be entitled to the G.I. Bill and wanted to take advantage of everything it offered. The bill would enable me to continue my education at a university and would provide for books, room, and board.

All in all, I worked in the dispensary for about nine months before I was discharged to go home to the States. Although I formed some close bonds with the men in the 12th General, I never reconnected with any of them at home. I hope that they all found happiness in life.

45. The Oldest Profession and Oldest Occupation (What a Soldier Does for Fun)

For the last four thousand years, one rule of men and war stands true: What does a soldier do for fun? A whorehouse.

I guess I was thinking like a desperate soldier. I had no idea how long this war was gonna last. What I did know was that I would need lots of money when I was discharged. I figured I could make tons of it if I owned a whorehouse. Lady Luck apparently agreed with this logic. One night while playing poker, I won $250 and decided to use it to bankroll my new little endeavor. I looked for a place to open one in Pusan, Korea, where I was stationed at the 12th General Dispensary.

The most available places were in the "off-limits" area designated by a large yellow sign with bold black letters. I found a vacant schoolhouse for rent for which I paid $150 a month. I divided the schoolhouse into fifty cribs (small private spaces) with hanging sheets. Each crib was furnished with a bed and two chairs.

I knew that I would have to have a full-time "madam" to control the operation while I was on duty. She would have to be beautiful, smart, and hopefully honest. I figured I would pay this woman a dollar for each girl who worked and another dollar for each "trick" a girl turned. The woman who I eventually hired found five hundred girls to work in my establishment.

Some of the girls she hired were previously streetwalkers or women who were unable to find other work. The girls often came from small towns on the Korean peninsula. We had a prolific supply of small-town girls who came looking for jobs and weren't able to find them, and so resorted to prostitution. Still others were former dance-hall girls who found it easier to work as prostitutes than to dance.

A girl was entitled to keep any money she could extract as a tip from a willing soldier. Very young and handsome women were paid $20 for a half hour of entertainment. Most of the girls were young and attractive, but a few were older and made up for what they lacked in youth and beauty by simulated passion. Some of the girls were "aristocratic looking" but were of humble families. Sadly, most were neither intelligent nor educated. The average working girl could earn between $250 and $500 a month. This was a lot of money back then.

My madam enthroned herself at the door where a cash register stood, charging each soldier $10 per trick. No man with $10 in his pocket was ever refused. Payment was in advance. After payment, she would ring a bell and any available girl would come forward to offer herself. They were quite competitive. Another in-house rule was that at the end of each session, a girl would bring a basin made of beer cans containing warm soapy water to her soldier and cleanse him.

As a medic, I was able to inspect each girl for venereal disease and treat her if any disease was present. The girls were inspected for their health monthly. The most common sexually transmitted diseases were gonorrhea, which is a gram-negative diplococci, cancroid, which is a gram-negative bacillus, and syphilis.

Before leaving camp, each soldier could obtain a "PR" kit furnished by the Army at no cost. Each contained a small bar of antibacterial soap, a penicillin tablet, a paper towel, a condom, and an instruction sheet. Upon leaving camp, the soldiers were always greeted by a bevy of women, some calling out, "Me sucky, me fuckee, your mother virgin."

All in all, I cleared $45,000 in the whorehouse business without lifting a finger. Perhaps a little of Whitey's criminal urge was in me back then. Maybe this money taught me a lesson. Maybe it's better if you decide. I'm still not sure.

46. Business Before Pleasure

The only people who had money in Korea from 1950 to 1952 were pimps, whores, politicians, and the military. They were all kind of the same. So I thought to myself, *Let's mix a little business and pleasure.*

You see, stylish clothes for the working girls were not available. If they had money to spend on nice clothes, they could look better. The better they looked, the more money they made.

My R&R was due. I had a choice of going to Sasebo, Kokura, or Tokyo for two weeks, to be paid for by the Army. I chose Sasebo because it had lots of shopping and was a fashion center.

When the troopships arrived in Japan from Korea, the American Army band greeted us by playing, "There'll Be a Hot Time in the Old Town Tonight." As we hit the gangplank, a chorus of girls offered their services. I looked for a hotel where I would stay the total time. I found a clean-looking hotel and negotiated the rent. Absolutely everything was negotiable.

I arrived a soldier without a girl at this hotel. So the hotel manager kept on sending girls to my room who not so shyly knocked at my door and offered their services. In a short half hour, I ended up rejecting nineteen girls. The manager then politely knocked at my door. Looking at the ground, hands in his pockets, his upper torso in a slight bow toward me, he asked if I would prefer a boy.

I bought a money belt before I left Korea in which I placed $5,000 and wore secured tightly to my body. With the money, I shopped for and bought fashionable dresses, lingerie, shoes, jewelry, coats, and cosmetics. I had the items wrapped in packages of $50 in value so that I would not have to pay customs tax and sent them back to my unit in Korea. I wouldn't have been able to accomplish this in two weeks. I would really need three weeks.

As luck would have it, a Communist riot broke out. I liked the timing. We US soldiers were detained in Kokura, and extra beds were required to house us. I was among those who volunteered to set up the beds and so I got my extra week. And by the way, it was paid for, and I got out of that damn hotel.

When I deplaned in Pusan, I was pulled aside by officers of the C.I.D. (Criminal Investigation Department). They claimed I was shipping contraband (liquor, ammunition, and weapons). I told them that I was sending gifts home to family and friends stateside. Up to this time, I had done nothing "illegal." They spoke to my CO (Commanding Officer), and it was decided that I would in the future notify him each time I sent an item home.

The items were to be secured in a Quonset hut. There were multiple rooms inside the hut, and each room had a locked door. The walls of each room, however, didn't extend to the ceiling of the hut, leaving a crawlspace at the top.

Subsequently, my CO was discharged to the States. This meant from my perspective that my CO "could not be contacted" about any shipment of my packages.

The rest was easy and made perfect sense. I hired a young Korean boy to go inside the Quonset hut. He'd climb up a ladder. He would then hop over the wall and slide down into each room, grab my gifts, and pass them back over the wall to me.

I sold the gifts on the black market. I doubled my money. Best of all, the C.I.D. never did find out what happened to the gifts.

47. What Happened With All That Money?

For every hundred dollars of military script, I could get only sixty dollars of good old American greenbacks on the Korean black market. After making the illegal exchange, I had about $45,000 that I planned to send home. I bought three volumes of the book "Gone with the Wind" and carefully placed crisp unused twenty-dollar bills between each page. Then I tightly wrapped each book with wrapping paper, scotch-taped it, tied it with string, and glued down just the right amount of postal stamps. I didn't insure the books because I figured it would raise some suspicion as to their value.

I mailed the books to my mother in Philadelphia. Oddly, she never acknowledged receiving the money-filled books to me or my brothers. As I found out much later, my aunt Lena, Mom's older sister, was advising her on what to do with the money. Aunt Lena was living in Los Angeles. She convinced Mom to move there and buy a three-bedroom house on her street, Cloverdale Avenue.

At that time, my brother Mike had been discharged from the Navy and was working as a cop in Philadelphia. Although he was living at home and was helping support Mom financially, she never consulted Mike as to whether or not to make the move to LA. In fact, she told him that he could make up his mind whether to move with her or in Philadelphia.

Mike never forgave Mom for this decision because he loved his work on the police force and was on the fast track to promotion. Nevertheless, feeling that he needed to protect his mother, he opted to move with her out west to LA.

My younger brother Lenny was still in the Navy when he heard about Mom's move to Los Angeles. He was happy and excited about it.

As for me, I never even heard of my mother's move since she never wrote me about it. Later, my cousin wrote to me and told me about the move to California. At first, I was indifferent. But then I figured that California might be just the right place to begin my life as a civilian.

48. The Homecoming

Hallelujah, I actually made it! The fighting was over for me. It was 1953. I sailed by troopship from Pusan to Seattle. While on board, I volunteered to be in the medical-hospital unit as a surgical nurse. I was allowed to do this because I had been trained as a medic. By doing this, I was given a regular bed to sleep in instead of having to sleep in a hammock like the rest of the enlisted men. I also could eat with the officers. Their food was much better.

I was expecting cheering crowds, waving flags, and brass bands playing military marches to welcome us home. There was nothing. There was not a soul to greet us as we marched off the gangplank. Boy, was I disappointed!

We were loaded onto a waiting bus and transported to Fort Lawton. There, we were detained for two days for indoctrination into normal civilian life.

One night while at Fort Lawton, I went to the world-famous Pike Place Market. I had been there before, before going overseas, and I thought it was a great place to revisit. Sitting at a bar, I met a beautiful young woman. With a shy smile, she offered to take me to a place that I hadn't seen for a long time. I was excited by her offer, and the two of us left the bar arm in arm, into a waiting chauffeured car.

We drove around Seattle through some beautiful neighborhoods and past lush green parks. To my surprise, the car pulled up in front of a gray stone church. She took me by the hand and led me to a recreation hall adjoining the church. Inside, there was music playing and lovely girls dancing with young men in uniform. Older women, their mothers I guessed, were serving sandwiches and soft drinks.

She introduced me to several pretty girls and then to the minister, who welcomed me warmly and thanked me for my service. At the end of the evening, all the soldiers were given rides back to their posts. I had a great time even though I had anticipated a different kind of fun.

After the two days of indoctrination, I was given my discharge papers and a paycheck to cover my expenses home. Although I had enlisted in Philadelphia and it was usual for discharged soldiers to return to the place they had entered the service, I asked to be discharged in Seattle because my family had moved to Los Angeles during the time I was overseas.

Someone told me that I would be paid to drive a rental car back to its place of origin. I talked to another soldier who was going to Los Angeles too. He agreed to share the driving with me and, of course, we would split the pay. It wasn't difficult to find a rental car agency that needed a car to be transported back to Los Angeles. All we needed was a valid driver's license. The agency would even provide insurance.

On the way home, I persuaded the other driver to make a quick stop in Sanger, California, to pay a condolence call at the home of the parents of John Tomkins. John was a buddy of mine who was killed by friendly fire at the Yalu River. John's mother greeted me with a lot of hostility. She never invited me in. She wanted to know why I was still living and her son was dead. I left rapidly, feeling guilty for being so lucky to be alive.

It took us two days to drive to Los Angeles. Someone from the rental agency drove me to 1845 South Cloverdale Street. This was where my mother had settled. Her house was down the street from her sister Lena. Everyone was really surprised to see me. Besides Mom, my brothers Mike and Lenny were there. My aunt Lena and uncle Maxie were also there. When they saw me, they all threw their arms around me and hugged me. I had tears in my eyes. I was overwhelmed by their outpouring of love. At last, I had the homecoming I'd been hoping for.

PART III: BECOMING – THE HONEST MAN WITHIN

49. Back to School

I was home safe and sound in Los Angeles, California, where my whole family had decided to settle. The house was a four-bedroom, one-story house. Mom had paid cash for the house, which was purchased with the money I'd made in Korea and had sent to her, as well as the proceeds from the sale of our home in Philadelphia.

I had made $100 for transferring the car from Seattle to Los Angeles, but I needed to find work right away. I had no trouble finding it. Back to the familiar, I would work as a grocery clerk at a Safeway market. Even though I had graduated with honors with a Bachelor of Science degree in chemistry from Temple University in Philadelphia, I wanted to continue my education. I wanted to use my G.I. bill, which would provide free tuition for graduate school.

I applied to UCLA, but the period for application had passed. So I applied for admission to USC, where admissions were still open, and I was accepted into the Department of Zoology. I felt like my future was beginning finally. But where I was headed, I was less sure.

I was paid fifty cents an hour as a grocery clerk. I told my Uncle Sam, who was a bookie in Los Angeles, what I was paid. He said that I must be nuts and that he would pay me two hundred dollars a week just for collecting bets on horse races. I quit my job at the grocery store and started to work as a bookie.

Booking bets was illegal. But I had to admit, the pay was good and it was easy work. Most of Uncle Sam's business had to do with horse racing. He had a shortwave radio and could get the results of a race directly from the track.

He knew how much money was won or lost before any of his

customers. Uncle Sam taught me how to make bets, give odds, and make payoffs. Bets were written on scraps of paper. If there was a chance of being caught by the police, we were told to eat the paper scraps pronto. I worked as a bookie for the time I was at USC. I was never arrested, but let me tell you, I did eat a lot of paper.

One of my favorite customers was Dr. Farber, who owned the Park View Hospital in Los Angeles. He took a liking to me, and we would often have long conversations. In a fatherly manner, he asked me what I wanted to do with my future. I said that I hadn't decided. That was when he suggested that I might like to become a medical doctor. In a flash, I thought to myself that that would be a great idea.

He said that if I wanted to apply to medical school, he would write a letter of recommendation for me to the University of California. This school was his alma mater and where he was now on the faculty.

So I ended up spending only one semester in graduate school at USC. School wasn't difficult for me. I took fifteen units in classes such as Advanced Zoology, Hematology, and Organic and Inorganic Chemistry. I still kept "making book" between classes using a car that I borrowed from Lennie.

My social life was great. There was a place on campus called The Grill where students hung out to eat and meet each other. I was older than most of the guys, and the girls seemed to like me. I was often invited to sorority parties and dances. I was also invited to campus activities such as plays, concerts, and sporting events. It was there that I met my future wife.

While still attending graduate school at USC, I applied and was accepted to medical school at the University of California. I would begin classes in the fall of 1953. The government benefits were great. The G.I. Bill paid for my tuition, books, room and board, and a small stipend for incidental living expenses.

That was when I quit my job as a bookie and became an honest man.

50. Meeting Nina at USC

The Grill was located in the basement of the student bookstore. Besides going there to eat and listen to the latest hit songs, guys and girls went there to meet each other. I would go there from time to time, grab a sandwich, and leave for class. Having lunch every day at The Grill was expensive for my allotment under the G.I. Bill.

Most of the time, I ate at the Hillel House, where students could meet and where food was free. The house was on campus on Hoover at 33rd Street and run by a student named Goldie. Goldie also served as the social director and introduced me to many girls, including one named Nina Levy. Nina was a sorority girl. She was a member of Alpha Epsilon Phi and a pharmacy student.

She had blond wavy hair and beautiful blue-green eyes. She had a lovely curvaceous figure, a vivacious personality, and was very smart. I later ran into her several times at The Grill and on campus but somehow never asked her out. One day I did call Nina. It was to get the telephone number of one of her friends, Bunny. She told me Bunny was out of town, so I asked Nina for a date to go to the horseraces.

I borrowed Lenny's car and picked Nina up in the late afternoon at her mother's house. Mike told me that the horses weren't running at Hollywood Park that day, so I took her out to dinner at Ed's, a popular steakhouse in West Hollywood.

After dinner, we strolled down Melrose Avenue looking at the shop windows and talking. We passed a small pet store that was open late. In the window, there was a flock of tiny, fluffy golden baby ducklings peeping and waddling around. We went into the store. I told Nina to pick out a duckling and that I would buy it for her. Nina was delighted and chose a goofy-looking ball of fuzz.

Our date went very well. I shared my experiences in the Army, and she told me of her work at a drugstore and her desire to become a pharmacist. Her father was a licensed pharmacist in Illinois who owned three pharmacies in Chicago. Our conversations flowed easily amid a lot of laughter. I took her home and kissed her goodnight, having enjoyed the evening immensely.

I continued to date other girls at USC, but I liked Nina the best. I knew she was dating other guys, too. In 1953, I started my studies in medical school at the University of California. To supplement my income, I worked at night as a caregiver at the homes of disabled patients.

Nina and I were dating each other exclusively by now. She was still at USC and working as a pharmacist's assistant. We saw each other whenever we could get away.

It was at about this time that my brothers and I decided to take back our legal family name of Koire. As youths, we had heard our grandfather proclaim that our family name had been changed to Cohen at Ellis Island by the immigration officer. This was not unusual, since immigration officials would often have trouble understanding foreign accents and unusual-sounding names and would bestow a new name on the newcomer. We were able to secure the ship's manifest, which proved this to be true. Mike hired a lawyer, who made the change official in court.

One night, Nina and I went out on a double date with Mike and his fiancée, Estelle. We drove to a romantic restaurant on the cliffs in Malibu overlooking the ocean. The waves swept softly over the rocks below us. Boy, was there music. Hoagy Carmichael, who happened to be a guest at the restaurant, was playing "Stardust" on the piano.

Nina looked beautiful in a brown lace dress with little brown flowers on it. I took her by the arm, and we walked to the edge of the patio overlooking the ocean. I asked her to marry me.

She smiled and gazed into my eyes. "Of course," she said.

51. Our Marriage

In 1954, Nina was still a student at the liberal arts college at USC in pre-pharmacy. Her father, a licensed pharmacist in Chicago, wanted her to get her pharmacy degree in California. His plan was to open a drugstore in Los Angeles where he would practice under her license.

When we decided to get married, Nina changed her major to education so that she could graduate within the year with a degree in teaching. Her father was disappointed in her decision because it ruined his plans. That was when he opposed her marriage to me, but that made no difference to Nina. On the other hand, Nina's mother was fond of me and sympathetic to her desire to get married.

Nina graduated from USC with honors in June of 1954 and found employment in the Compton School District as a kindergarten teacher. We were married on the eighth of August of that year. Our wedding took place at a small temple on Santa Monica Blvd. in West Los Angeles.

We had about a hundred guests, family, and friends. My brother Mike was the best man. Nina looked beautiful as she walked down the aisle in her white gown trimmed with a baby-blue sash. She was escorted by her father, who gave her away.

The rabbi, unknown to us before, was from South Africa and spoke with such a thick accent that neither of us could understand him. It was only after I traditionally stomped on the wine glass and after all of our guests shouted "Mazel Tov" that we knew we were married.

After the wedding ceremony, the room was set up for dinner and dancing. The orchestra was led by Larry Wolf, who was an old boyfriend of Nina's. The band had an outstanding trumpet player, Herb Alpert, who would soon become famous as the leader of the band Tijuana Brass.

At the end of the evening, as Nina and I left amid a shower of rice, tears from her parents, and shouts of good wishes from our friends, we headed to the Beverly Carlton Hotel in Beverly Hills (now the Avalon), where we began our lives together.

The following morning, we headed north to Lake Tahoe for our honeymoon. We traveled in a new Chevy Bel Air that Nina's father had supposedly given us as a wedding present but was still in his name. I didn't have much money and was on a tight budget, so I could only afford to spend ten dollars a night for a motel room. If the room cost more, I would plead with the clerk, saying that I was on my honeymoon and could only afford ten dollars. They all were very sympathetic and let us stay for that price.

We planned to be away for two weeks. During that time, we explored beautiful Lake Tahoe and its surrounding pine forests. We stopped off at the Mapes Hotel in Reno, Nevada, which had a huge and luxurious casino but where I did no gambling. Behind the Mapes Hotel in this city famous for its quick divorces was the Truckee River, into which newly divorced women were rumored to have thrown their wedding rings.

We proceeded on to San Francisco, where I splurged for a night and reserved a room at the elegant Mark Hopkins Hotel on Nob Hill. We dined and danced that evening while admiring the sparkling lights of the city below.

The following day, after briefly exploring the city, we headed home, driving along the Pacific coast. We stopped for a few hours to explore the magnificent Hearst Castle, admiring its elaborate rooms, spectacular swimming pool, and sumptuous grounds with its private zoo.

We made our home on Kings Road in Ladera Heights, living with Nina's mother, who was separated from her father. Then we began our married life together. I returned to my classes at medical school and to my full-time evening shift as a nurse at Las Campanas Hospital. I took on the financial responsibility of the house. Nina returned to her teaching.

52. My Summer with Charlie Randal

In the summer of my second year of medical school, 1954, I got a job as the caretaker for Charlie Randal. He was a patient at Compton Sanitarium and had been placed there because of a brain injury.

Charlie had been employed as a steam fitter. He was working at a plant installing a boiler when the ladder he was standing on collapsed. He fell to the concrete floor below and hit his head, which knocked him unconscious. He was taken by ambulance to Las Campanas, where an X-ray diagnosed him as having a subdural hematoma. Multiple surgeries to stop the bleeding were unsuccessful. The bleeding finally stopped spontaneously but left him with a brain deficit.

His family placed him in Compton Sanitarium, which was a respected institution for mentally ill patients. All of Charlie's hospitalization and medical expenses including salary for a caregiver, were paid for by workmen's comp.

Charlie could no longer care for himself. He needed someone to bathe him, dress him, shave him, and watch over him in general. He was a heavy cigarette smoker but would burn his fingers if he wasn't reminded to put the cigarette out.

Taking care of Charlie was my only responsibility at the sanitarium. I took care of him in the evening and overnight. Charlie was a small man and slightly built. He was frail-looking and pale, with grayish, thinning hair. But Charlie had a twinkle in his eyes. He was pleasant company and liked to play jokes.

At night, I would sleep on the floor in front of the door of Charlie's room. The room was never locked. Occasionally, however, he would manage to sneak out and get around me to the door. He liked taking walks about the grounds at night.

On one such evening, he decided to leave the sanitarium on one of his walks. He accidentally woke me, so I followed him closely, trying to convince him to return to the hospital grounds, but he insisted he wanted to go for a beer. I didn't want to force him to return because I was afraid I would hurt him. He just seemed so fragile. So we both walked together until we reached the Kitty-Kat Bar a few blocks away and went inside.

Charlie stepped up to the bar. Like nobody's business, he said, "Give me a Bud."

The bartender handed him a small glass of beer and some peanuts on a plate. "That's a dollar," said the barkeep.

I pulled a dollar out of my pocket and handed it to him. Charlie guzzled down the beer with a smile on his face and said, "Let's go."

We walked down Compton Blvd. Charlie led the way, going farther away from the sanitarium. At Rosecrans Blvd., there was a stoplight. Traffic was heavy. We stopped. I tried to convince him to turn around and return to the sanitarium. He would have no part of that. He started to push me, so I carefully wrestled him to the ground.

"Help! Help!" yelled Charlie to the passing cars. "This guy's trying to kill me!"

Someone must have called the police, for in a few minutes a cruiser arrived with sirens blaring. Out jumped two cops with guns drawn.

"What's going on here?" one of them asked.

With Charlie still yelling, "He's trying to kill me!" and me trying to hold him down, I explained to the police exactly what had happened. I let them know I worked at Compton Sanitarium as his caregiver. The officers called the sanitarium to confirm my story, after which they drove us back in the squad car.

Charlie often talked about "our little adventure" while laughing out loud. "I guess I played a joke on you," he would say.

"The joke's on you, Charlie," I'd reply, laughing. "No more outings for beer."

I worked as Charlie's caregiver for about a year. I left because I got another job. The hours were better for me since I was attending medical school full-time. Then, about a year after I left, I got a phone call from Charlie's family. He had passed away. Charlie still makes me smile.

53. Becoming a Father

We were young, happy, busy, and in love. I was in my junior year at medical school and still holding down a full-time job taking care of Charlie. Nina was teaching third-grade students at Compton Elementary School.

One afternoon while at school, I got a call from the principal of Nina's school. "Please come and pick up your wife," he said. "She's not feeling well. She's nauseous and has been vomiting."

I hurried as fast as I could, picking up my brother Lenny along the way so that he could drive Nina's car home. I was at her school within the hour. I drove her to her doctor's office on Sunset Boulevard and Gardner. After examining Nina, the doctor called me into his office and told me I was going to be a father.

Nina and I were delighted. It didn't matter to us if the baby was a boy or a girl, so long as it was healthy. The baby was due to be born in September 1955.

Nina was a real trooper. The first few months of her pregnancy were difficult. She was often sick to her stomach. I frequently had to pick her up from school to bring her home because of her morning sickness.

There wasn't a morning that she didn't get up, get dressed, and go to school. The principal of her school was very supportive. He even changed her assignment from third grade to kindergarten, hoping that teaching younger students would be less stressful.

After a while, the pregnancy became easier, and on September 5, 1955, at Maywood Hospital, the baby was born. It was a girl, and we named her Alison Sonja.

Alison was a strong, healthy baby, adorable, with blond curls and blue eyes. She was smart, too, learning to walk and talk at an early age. Nina and

I had fun playing with her. Nina's mother, who took care of her while I was at school and Nina was teaching, loved to put huge white bows in Alison's hair.

"Like they do in Russia," her grandmother would happily say.

Finally, in June of 1957, I completed medical school. I graduated second in my class. The graduation ceremony was held at the Pasadena Civic Auditorium. My whole family was there: Nina, my brothers and their wives, Mom, and Nina's mother. Of course, two-year-old Alison was there, too. Nina had her clothed in a white ruffled dress with a gigantic white bow clipped to her bouncy yellow curls.

As I paraded down the aisle, I saw her little blond head pop up like a flower in a field. She pointed to me and said in a very loud but sweet voice, "There's my daddy!"I couldn't have been more proud.

54. My First Internship

I had to apply for a year of internship right after completing four grueling years in medical school. The finest internship in the country was at Los Angeles County Hospital. The sheer volume of patients that were treated there was astounding. There were three thousand hospital beds in the facility.

It was the teaching hospital for three medical schools: USC, Loma Linda, and the College of Osteopathic Physicians and Surgeons. The hospital had twenty-seven units, a few of which included Pediatrics, Contagious Diseases, Orthopedics, Surgery, Tuberculosis, Maternity, and Emergency Medicine. Being second in my graduating class almost guaranteed me a position as an intern there. LA County Hospital was the only internship for which I applied, and I was accepted.

At that time, interns were paid a salary of $225 a month, given room and board, and supplied with hospital clothing and laundry service. We interns each had a schedule that told us where to be and at what time to be there. We worked sixteen hours a day but were on call twenty-four hours a day and every other weekend.

Our living quarters, which we called Shangri-La, were on the hospital grounds and next to the laundry facility, from where we heard the swishing of the washing machines and the hissing of the presses day and night.

Underneath the hospital complex was a system of tunnels that connected all the buildings so that one could go anywhere on the campus without having to go outside. All food, supplies, and equipment were transported through these tunnels, which were so large that two cars could pass through side by side.

We were very busy taking care of patients, of which there were plenty.

LA County was serving a population that was approaching five million people. We had a saying: "Nobody falls out of bed in the County Hospital, they fall into the next bed."

Not only were there patients to see who were in the hospital, but there were also patients to see in the clinics as outpatients. Sometimes the wait to see a doctor was so long in the clinics that the hospital would provide lunch or even dinner.

This was the height of the post-war baby boom. The maternity ward offered great opportunities to learn and practice. In my six-week rotation there, I delivered 154 babies and one set of twins.

The senior resident, Dr. Joe Young, was a wonderful teacher who allowed us to do complicated obstetrical procedures like forceps deliveries or difficult vaginal repairs while carefully monitoring us.

I especially enjoyed the general surgery rotation because I learned so much. We observed and could sometimes assist in surgeries such as bowel resections or appendectomies. We were questioned by the attending surgeon about the physiology and chemistry of the procedure, and about post-op care. We were given a lot of responsibilities but were very closely supervised.

The competition among the interns was keen. We were the brightest of the bright. We all tried to impress the attending staff. They would be the ones who would choose the residents and their specialties for the coming year.

Even though I was on call, in my off hours I worked in East Los Angeles at an emergency hospital. Nina and I had little Alison to care for, and we needed the extra money.

One night at the emergency hospital, a man walked in who had been shot in the shoulder. I told him I had to report any bullet wound to the police.

The man pulled out a knife and threatened to stab me if I didn't take the bullet out. So I had a nurse prep him for surgery.

When he was lying on the table, I took a long surgical knife, put it to his throat, and said, "You son of a bitch, what are you going to do now?"

He threw off the surgical sheet and ran out of the hospital. I reported the incident to the police, but I never told anyone at County Hospital that I had an outside job for fear of losing my internship.

55. My Residency: Expect the Unexpected

"Hey, Art. Why wasn't I selected for an orthopedic residency?" I asked.

Dr. Art Miller bowed his head and told me that Dr. Girard thought there were already too many Jews in the orthopedic department. Art was not only my friend but a member of the faculty who was on the board that selected orthopedic residents. But Dr. Girard was chairman of the board, and he always had the final word.

During my year of internship, the two fields I thought were the most interesting and that I wanted to pursue in my residency were orthopedics and general surgery. Orthopedics was my favorite at that point in time. I was an excellent intern, one of the best and brightest in our class, and so I was stunned by not being chosen.

Instead, I was accepted to my second choice as a general surgery resident. This area would offer me the opportunity to go into many other surgical sub-specialties such as hand surgery, burns, congenital deformities, plastic and reconstructive and cosmetic surgery.

On the first day of my job, I was assigned to the gynecological surgical clinic, where I was to examine a patient. She complained of a vaginal mass and a malodorous discharge. As I walked into the examination room, a nurse dressed properly in her white uniform and cap was spraying the air with a can of odor repellant in one hand and holding her nose with the other. I asked her for a pair of gloves, and she gloved me.

I asked the patient how long she'd had this condition, and she replied that it had started about a month before and had gotten worse. I proceeded to examine her and found the large mass of which she was complaining. It was about six by four inches and was not of human tissue.

I used a tenaculum, an instrument with four teeth, to remove it from her vagina. Lo and behold! It was a sprouting sweet potato. As I held the offending object in the air, my patient looked at it and said, "I wonder how that got in there!"

One night after midnight, I was called to the emergency room. There was a young man in his twenties lying on a gurney. His pants were bloody at the crotch, and he was moaning and obviously in a lot of pain. I lowered his pants and saw a ballpoint pen filler within the shaft of his penis.

I asked him what had happened, and he told me that he couldn't get an erection. He said that his partner suggested using the ballpoint pen filler as a solution to their problem.

We wheeled him into surgery. I anesthetized his penis and successfully removed the ballpoint pen filler and put a catheter in place to assist in healing.

An hour later, I returned to check on my patient, who was now peacefully sleeping in his room. There, pinned to his blanket, was a note placed by some prankster. It read, "If you can't come, write!"

Dr. Joe Young was the chief resident in gynecological surgery. On one day, he had thirty-one deliveries and was overwhelmed. He had a patient who needed a third-degree repair, which is a post-delivery repair of a tear from the vagina to the rectum. He asked his interns if anyone knew how to do this type of repair. One enthusiastic intern volunteered.

Afterward, when Dr. Young checked the incision, he discovered that the intern had sewn everything closed, including the rectum and vagina. He then paged me down to the operating room to fix the botched surgery and to demonstrate to the interns the correct way of doing a third-degree repair.

Although there were unusual, humorous, or even bizarre situations we residents experienced in our first year, we all worked hard and were determined to become the best doctors that we could be.

56. The Highland Park Incident

I was in the first year of my surgical residency at the Los Angeles County Hospital. In June 1959, I was invited to attend the graduation and capping of the forty-one women who had completed the registered nursing program. Most of the house staff attended. The ceremony was held in the large hospital auditorium.

While in training, most of the nurses lived in Highland Park in a three-building wooden apartment complex because the rent was cheap and it was located near the hospital. That evening, the nurses planned a celebration party at their living quarters. They invited the male residents and interns of the house staff. They planned an evening of music, dancing, and refreshments. Of course, there would be plenty of booze.

I was on call that evening, so I didn't plan to go to the party. As it happened, I had three emergency surgeries: a ruptured appendix with peritonitis, a subdural hematoma, and a ruptured ovarian cyst.

Milt Perlow, who was my anesthesiologist that evening, and I finished our surgeries at about 11:00 p.m. Shortly thereafter, we received a call from the nurses at Highland Park begging us to join them in the fun. We decided to go.

We made arrangements with the emergency room physician to call us if we were needed. Still in our scrubs, we jumped into Milt's Chevy convertible and drove to the party. The party was in full swing when we arrived. Not only was the hospital staff there, but some uninvited residents of the compound had crashed the party. Milt and I weren't drinking because we were still on call, but we enjoyed the food and conversation.

One of the nurses came up and grabbed me by the arm. "Dr. Koire, we need your help." She whispered this as she dragged me toward the back bedroom. "Cathy has passed out, and one of the crashers is trying to rape her!"

As I entered the bedroom, I saw Cathy, unconscious and stark naked, lying face down on the bed. The intruder was about to rape her.

I grabbed the intruder by his pants and dragged him to the front door. I shoved him out onto a wooden railing by the door, which broke under the impact, and sent him sprawling on the ground. He jumped up and, as he ran toward his apartment, yelled, "I'll be back."

A few minutes later, he returned with four comrades carrying knives and baseball bats and rushed into the nurses' apartment. He ran up to me with a bat in his hands as I was standing by the bar, threatening to get me.

I reached back on the bar and grabbed a bottle of whiskey. I broke it on the bar sink and pointed the sharp end toward him, saying, "Not 'til I kill two of you."

The intruder stopped short. "This guy is crazy," he shouted to his companions. "Let's get out of here!"

One of the nurses had called the police, who arrived shortly afterward. By that time, the crashers had disappeared. By then, so had we. Milt Perlow and I returned to the hospital, exhausted.

The following day, I was called into the office of Dr. O'Meara, who was the director of the residents' program. "I heard you were quite the hero last night," he said. "Maybe we should start calling you John Wayne."

I was thinking of denying the whole incident for fear of being dismissed from my residency. But before I could reply, he continued. "I really want to thank you for taking care of one of our nurses. If it weren't for you, she could have been seriously hurt."

57. Along Came Hillary

On July 19, 1960, our second daughter was born. Hillary made the Koire family complete. She was born at the old Cedars of Lebanon Hospital on Fountain Avenue in Los Angeles. Nina and I were delighted that Alison would have a little sister. We named her Hillary Suzanne. Like her older sister, she was blond, blue-eyed, and adorable.

We brought Hillary home to our new home on Shenandoah in Ladera Heights. Nina's mother was still living with us and taking care of the children while Nina was out teaching. I was in my second year of surgical residency at the County Hospital. All seemed to be going well.

When Hillary was about one, on a routine visit to her pediatrician, the doctor noticed that her legs were not developing normally. The leg bones from the knees to the ankles were twisted. This condition is called tibia torsion. If not corrected, Hillary would walk pigeon-toed for the rest of her life.

The pediatrician recommended we take her to an orthopedic surgeon, and we did. He was Dr. Bornstein, a medical school classmate of mine. Dr. Bornstein put Hillary's legs in casts from the knee to the ankle. He told us that we would have to twist her legs and rotate them into the proper position. This, we would have to do twice a day. He showed Nina and me the correct way to do the manipulation. Hillary screamed and cried. The procedure was extremely painful.

Neither Nina nor her mother could bear to do this manipulation. They couldn't stand to cause Hillary pain or hear her screams. So it was up to me to twist her legs so that eventually, they would grow straight and strong.

It got to a point where Hillary would scream in terror when she heard my voice or saw me enter a room. My mere presence terrified her. When she was in her crib and I approached, she would cower in a corner with her back toward me and wail in heartbreaking sobs. All of this hurt me to the core, and I felt extreme guilt for causing her so much pain. As much as I hated to do this procedure, I knew that I had to.

Hillary had to wear the casts and endure those awful exercises for a whole year. When Dr. Bornstein was finally able to remove the casts, he was pleased with the result. Her legs were perfect, and she walked with her toes pointed straight ahead.

It took a long time for my daughter to get over her fear of me. As the months passed and she no longer had to endure the pain, her trust in me grew. She became my affectionate and fun-loving little girl. But to this day, she can recall quite vividly what she suffered.

58. House Calls: Poor Joe Brown

"Operator, I need a doctor as soon as possible. There's a man convulsing here!"

I needed to work, so as soon as I got my medical license and was able to practice, I joined a service that enabled doctors to make house calls for a flat rate charge of $25. One night, I was awakened at 10:30 by the service to make a house call on South Figueroa Avenue where a patient was convulsing with a high fever and cough.

When I arrived at the address, which turned out to be a hotel, there were people standing outside on the street who directed me to the lobby where the patient was lying on the floor and convulsing. I immediately placed two tongue depressor blades, wrapped together with tape, into his mouth so that he wouldn't swallow his tongue.

I took his blood pressure, which was high at 250 over 180. Then I listened to his chest, which sounded congested, with deep-rough rales. Rales are a crackling sound upon inhaling and are a sure sign of trouble in the lungs.

The pupils of his eyes were dilated. I took off his shirt and put a tourniquet on his right upper arm. Then I proceeded to fill a syringe with 25mg of Thorazine and injected it slowly into the brachial vein.

The patient slowly stopped convulsing. He opened his eyes, and in a few minutes sat up and asked for a cigarette. The crowd, who had gathered around to watch, was astounded. They clapped loudly.

I put my medical equipment back into my bag and told the desk clerk that the company would bill the patient, whose name was Joe Brown. I stood up proudly and instructed the desk clerk to take the man to his bed and to make him comfortable. I wrote two prescriptions to be filled later by Mr. Brown and headed for my car.

As I walked down the front steps, I heard someone scream, "Doctor! Doctor, come back! He's convulsing again!"

I rushed back in two steps at a time, straight to the lobby. There, as before, lay Joe Brown on the floor, convulsing. Again, I placed the tourniquet onto his right upper arm and slowly gave him a second dose 25mg of Thorazine. He responded quickly, stopping his convulsions. That was also when he stopped breathing.

I performed CPR to no avail. I couldn't resuscitate him for the life of me. The ever-present crowd began to whisper among themselves. "He killed him!!!"

After protesting my innocence to the crowd, I called the city coroner. First I called to report the death of my patient, and then to be reassured that I had done everything that was medically correct.

When the ambulance came to carry the body away to the city coroner's office, I heard the desk clerk mumble, "I guess good old Joe Brown won't be paying his bill."

And then there was that simple flu case. I arrived in the early evening at an apartment house in the barrios of Los Angeles. The building was ill-kempt, dismal, and filthy. As I walked up the stairs to the second floor, I could hear the boards creaking beneath my feet. I walked along the dimly lit hall and knocked at the door.

The patient was an attractive young woman in her twenties. When she opened the door and turned on the lights, I could see and hear cockroaches scratching the floor as they scrambled for dark hiding places.

She complained of aching bones, a cough, and fever, all symptoms of the flu. Her lungs were clear. I gave her an injection of an antibiotic and a prescription for pain pills. She paid her bill, and I left.

A few months later, I was called back to her apartment. When she opened the door, she was stark naked and smiling. She invited me in.

"Would you like a cup of coffee?" she said. "After that, we can have some fun."

She assured me she was feeling fine. I could hear a man's voice coming from her bedroom. After four years of university, four years of medical school, a year of internship, and seven years of residency, I knew I wasn't supposed to be stupid.

"Adios," I said as I spun around and got the hell out of there.

59. Cosmetic Surgery

In 1962, cosmetic surgery was not considered a serious branch of medicine.

There were very few places to get training in this field. Training was offered as a preceptorship in a doctor's office but not in an accredited program at a medical school.

It wasn't until 1986 that the Board of Cosmetic Surgery was established and approved by the American Medical Association (AMA). After that, a doctor could become a certified cosmetic surgeon if he submitted a record of his surgical caseloads to the Board for its approval and passed an oral and written examination.

After completing four years of residency in general surgery, I became interested in pursuing a career in cosmetic surgery. I was attracted to the creative and artistic possibilities in this field. Even as a youth, I liked to paint with watercolors and carve wood.

While trying to figure out this attraction to the arts, I was reminded of the time when one of my wood carvings of an Indian was placed on exhibition at the Philadelphia Museum of Art in the children's division.

It was especially difficult to schedule cosmetic procedures at a hospital. They were not considered essential. They were always categorized as elective and therefore of secondary priority. They were always scheduled or slipped in after all the other surgeries were completed. That is the reason, even today, why most plastic surgeons have approved surgical theaters in their offices or operate in surgical centers that aren't located in hospitals.

As I began to search for a cosmetic surgeon who offered training, I discovered that there were very few who were willing to teach this specialty. Eventually, I was accepted into an approved program offered by a well-known surgeon in Los Angeles, without pay. The doctor had two surgical theaters in his office and was rather busy. He meant business. His preceptorship was to last for two years, after which I would take an examination for certification by the Cosmetic Board (although it wasn't yet approved by the AMA).

The years that I was with him were the most humiliating of my life. Although I learned many cosmetic procedures, he referred to me as his "boy."

I was never permitted to be with him during his consultations with patients. He would often send me on his personal errands like picking up his laundry or filling his car with gas.

Although I handled all of his emergency calls at night and attended to all of his hospital patients, he would berate me in front of the patients by criticizing my choice of procedures.

One time, after I had been there for a year and a half, the doctor broke his wrist in a car accident and was unable to operate for six weeks. Finally, I got the chance to prove myself. I did all the surgeries and did a good job. But of course, he would never praise me.

When the doctor had recovered and was able to operate again, the first thing that he did was dismiss me from the program. He told me he didn't want me in the office anymore, and that he thought I was too arrogant. I was furious.

I had no trouble finding work doing surgery for other physicians, but I was not yet certified in cosmetic surgery and wanted to finish the program. I had a year and a half of my life invested. So I swallowed what was left of my pride and went back to my preceptor and asked him to let me finish the program. In fact, I begged. He let me reenter the program, and I finished the last six months without incident.

I passed my certification exam and soon opened an office at 9255 Sunset Boulevard in Beverly Hills. I was very busy and became involved in medical politics. I was elected president of the American Breast Society.

Sometimes fate has a funny way. One evening, a patient called me with an emergency. She was a patient of my old nemesis, my old preceptor. He had operated on her nose, and it had begun to bleed profusely.

It was after midnight, and the doctor didn't want to get out of bed to treat it. He told her to call me. I told the patient that she should call her surgeon back and that I was sure he would be glad to take care of it.

I thought to myself, *This 'boy' doesn't have to do his bidding anymore.*

60. The Crash on the 405

I opened my eyes suddenly from the darkness of my unconsciousness to see sparks flying like a Fourth of July display. I felt and heard my car crash and scrape as it careened along the chain-link fence that divided the 405 freeway. Eighty-six yards of freeway fence was torn up and destroyed before my car limped to a stop. And then, silence. I had fallen asleep while driving, and the shock of the impact had awakened me.

"I think he's dead!" I heard the voice of a woman cry out.

I couldn't move. I was pinned to the seat by my seat belt and by the twisted dashboard and collapsed steering wheel of my maroon 1959 Thunderbird convertible.

"I'm not dead!" I yelled. "Get me the hell out of here!"

Two hours earlier, at 11:00 p.m., I was still at my new office on Sunset Boulevard, finishing up my day with an emergency surgery. A man had fallen off a ladder at his home and had cut his face badly and broken his nose. The man was a previous patient and had called me when his accident happened at eight o'clock in the evening, asking for me to wait for him.

Just as I finished the operation, I got a telephone call from Dr. Roger Thill, who had referred many patients to me in the past. He had an emergency patient, a longshoreman, who had gotten into a knife fight at the docks and received many lacerations of the face, body, and extremities. His patient was hospitalized at Little Company of Mary and scheduled for surgery at 2:00 a.m. Dr. Thill asked me to do the surgery. Even though I was tired, I agreed. I didn't want to disappoint him.

Back at the crash, crowds of people and cars had stopped and gathered around me. Someone must have called the fire department using a freeway call box because soon I heard the sound of sirens approaching. I was happy to hear them. I was afraid the Thunderbird would catch fire and explode.

When the firemen arrived, they carefully examined the crash. They asked me how I was. I looked around, seeing the twisted metal and shattered glass. Except for a broken nose, a broken finger, and small pieces of glass embedded in my face and chest, I was okay. I was lucky. The firemen estimated that, with my heavy foot on the accelerator, I was going over 125 miles an hour when I hit the chain-link divider.

After trying and failing to extricate me from the wreck, one of the firemen said, "We have to use the jaws of life to get you out of this mess."

The jaws of life are piston-driven hydraulic tools that are cutters, spreaders, and rams. They're used to cut through thick pieces of metal. The firemen worked for an hour. Finally, I was taken from the wreck.

When the ambulance arrived to take me to the hospital, I asked them to take me to Little Company of Mary. You can Imagine Dr. Thill's surprise when he saw me wheeled into the emergency room. He was still waiting for me to operate on the longshoreman.

We decided that my injuries would be cared for first, with Dr. Thill doing the surgery and me supervising. Next, we would tend to the longshoreman, again with Dr. Thill operating and me supervising.

Dawn was coming by the time we finished. I called a cab to take me home. When I arrived, my family was sound asleep. It wasn't until morning that they heard about my crash on the 405.

What a night!!!

PART IV: THE PLACES I'VE GONE – THE PEOPLE I'VE MET AND SERVED

61. Albert Schweitzer (1875-1965)

In the summer of 1963, I accepted a fellowship at the Albert Schweitzer Hospital in Gabon, in west Central Africa. I was interested in working with Dr. Schweitzer because he had been a Nobel Prize winner in 1952 for his philosophy of "Reverence for Life." He was a true renaissance man and thrived as a theologian, philosopher, and physician.

The philosophy led to the founding of this hospital in what was at the time French Equatorial Africa. He was, during my fellowship, doing mostly supervisory work.

When I arrived, I was shown the medical compound, which was like a village and completely surrounded by jungle. In the center was a large hospital made of wood that resembled a large barn.

Dr. Schweitzer's wife, Helene Bresslau, was born in Berlin in 1879 to a cultivated family of assimilated Jews. She was an active anesthesiologist when I was there, as well as a registered nurse and an experienced social worker. She was intelligent, independent-minded, and in possession of a highly-developed social conscience.

This building, I discovered, was built by the labor of the natives and by patients. It was for the care of Black patients only. Nearby, in the compound, was the hospital for white patients only. Although it was smaller, it was made of brick and appeared to be much stronger.

Schweitzer and his wife lived here in a mid-sized brick cottage. The doctors and nurses lived in separate dormitories, which were primitive with outdoor plumbing and had no running water. In the compound were also small vegetable gardens tended by "the natives."

I soon learned of the types of diseases that were prevalent in Equatorial Africa. We treated yaws, syphilis, sleeping sickness, malaria, and anemia.

We also treated burns and cleft palates and harelips. Insect and spider bites were common, too, and could be serious, carrying poisons and infections. Out of the six fellows while I was there, two came down with malaria. Schweitzer himself suffered from anemia and type 2 diabetes (he cured himself).

At night amid the rising howls of lions, hyenas, and other wild animals just as we were trying to fall asleep, the air was filled with the profound sound of organ music. Schweitzer was a renaissance man and a world-class organist. He even had an electric organ shipped from Europe and reassembled in his cottage. He played nightly, preferring Bach and his own compositions. His playing, although professionally rendered, kept the other animals and me awake.

The presence of wild animals was always a problem in this jungle compound. Baboons would come through the open windows of the dormitories and steal anything that wasn't locked up and put away. They were vicious and bite if someone struggled to take back a stolen object. There were old hunters, expert marksmen, stationed at the perimeter of the compound, ready to shoot any hostile, invading beast.

I saw Albert Schweitzer daily during my one-month fellowship. He was a gruff and grouchy old man who was more interested in expounding his philosophy than teaching us fellows the principles of tropical medicine. All of his doctors, residents, and fellows were Caucasian. This was at the height of apartheid.

This world-famous philosopher and doctor wasn't interested in training any Blacks to be medical staff doctors. I found him offensive in his racist comments. He felt the natives of Gabon were too uneducated and simple to run an independent nation, and that it would prosper more under European control. He looked upon Africans as "children" who needed his care and supervision—the white man's burden.

Ironically, his philosophy—his "Reverence for Life"—included a tenderness for all living creatures including insects. We were often warned to be careful where we walked so as not to step on a passing bug.

The hospitals, both for Blacks and whites, were inadequate compared to American standards but were the best they had in the region. The patients in both hospitals were treated equally. The equipment was antiquated and the medicine in short supply.

After a month, when my service was finished, I returned home disappointed in my fellowship with Albert Schweitzer. Although I didn't mind the long hours and hard work, I felt I had learned very little from my efforts, and I was upset by the bigotry of the leader of this program.

Later, I learned that Dr. Schweitzer had passed away at the age of ninety in Gabon, two years after my fellowship. The fellowship program is still offered at the Albert Schweitzer Hospital.

62. Ethiopia Calling

It was a bright sunny day when, flying from London on British Airways, we landed at Addis Ababa, the capital of Ethiopia. The "we" was a group of doctors on a sightseeing trip to Ethiopia. The trip was not only for pleasure, but also to visit a hospital in the country where we were scheduled to surgically correct cleft palates, and our group's ophthalmologists to remove cataracts.

We were met at the terminal by the minister of health. As we left the airport, we were greeted by the symbol of the country, a huge black-maned lion. The poor creature was leashed and led by its trainer. When it opened its mouth to yawn, we could see that it was toothless. Everyone wanted to take a picture with the beast.

Our group of thirty doctors was taken by bus to a hotel that seemed more like a garage, clean but primitive. We were warned that electricity, running water, and air conditioning were only available from eight in the morning to four in the afternoon. We would have to make do with flashlights at night.

The following afternoon, we were invited to lunch with the emperor of Ethiopia, "The Lion of Judah" Haile Selassie, at his palace. As we approached the stately neoclassical structure on our private bus, we passed by the emperor's gardens and private zoo where he kept animals from all over Africa, including the rare black-maned lion.

Arriving, we were led into a large columned reception room where we were greeted by the emperor. He was a small, slender, frail-looking man. Standing next to the emperor was his son. He was tall, heavyset, and considered to be the oldest prince who never became king. The emperor shook each of our hands and thanked us for coming. After a lunch of cucumber sandwiches and wine, we went back to our hotel.

Gondar was next on our itinerary. The small white church was surrounded by a wrought iron fence and was guarded day and night. No one except the guard, who lived at the church, was allowed to enter either the church itself or the small sanctuary wherein the Ark of the Covenant— which supposedly holds the stone tablets of the Ten Commandments given on Mount Sinai by God to Moses—was said to rest. The bus stopped at the church, and the guard waved to us. This was the closest we ever got to the sacred relic.

It was in Gondar, at a local hospital, where we doctors were scheduled to do surgery. It was a small hospital, perhaps fifty beds, but clean, although lacking in the most modern equipment. We each operated on one or two patients and were assisted by local doctors.

Nearby Gondar are villages of Falasha Jews. We went to visit a Falasha village one day. Falashas are Black Jews who claim to be direct descendants of the patriarch Abraham who practice an ancient form of Judaism.

On the same day we visited the Falasha village, we went to explore the underground churches built by ancient Christians on the plains near Gondar. The churches were carved out of solid rock and were built below ground to hide from the marauding Arab Muslims.

As I descended the carved stone steps into the chapel, I saw pictures of the Stations of the Cross, martyred saints, and Christian symbols etched into the walls. Ethiopian Christian monks offered translations of the carved symbols and writings for a donation.

We traveled throughout Ethiopia for around two weeks learning about a poor but proud people. We enjoyed sampling the local food, especially injera, a spongy flatbread Ethiopians use at every meal in place of flatware to scoop up their flavorful and spicy dishes. Every evening, we listened to lectures about the history and culture of the country. Sometimes, we were entertained by local singers and dancers.

When our trip was over, our group was transported back to Addis Ababa by limousine for our flight back to London.

63. A Close Call and Lesson in Parenting

In 1964, my family—Nina, Alison, Hillary, and I—were living in Ladera Heights, which was a friendly, upscale neighborhood in Los Angeles not far from the ocean or LAX. Back then, residents of this neighborhood were mostly young married couples with children. Many were professionals: physicians, dentists, and attorneys. Others were merchants who owned their own businesses or were engineers who had manufacturing companies.

Nina and I bought a house on South Halm Avenue, a modern one-story home with a white stone facade. It had four bedrooms and a swimming pool and was built around a large atrium. There was a wrought iron sculpted fountain in the center of the atrium, around which flowers and plants bloomed year-round, changing with the seasons.

The house had a three-car garage. In one of the spaces, I had installed a gymnasium, something I always wanted. On one wall, I hung a boxer's speed bag. In the center, I placed weightlifting equipment. It was a well-equipped gym with benches and weight racks. I worked out three times a week.

One day, six-year-old Hillary came into the gym while I was working out. She greeted me as she always did, with a smile and a kiss. As we chatted and she told me about her day at school, she walked around the gym, touching pieces of equipment here and there as I continued to work out.

She took down my jump rope from its place on the wall and began to jump, singing, "Down by the river, down by the sea, Johnny broke a bottle and blamed it on me." She put down the rope and then eyed my workout bench with a two-hundred-pound barbell resting on a rack over it.

I wasn't looking at her when, for some reason, Hillary thought it would be fun to do a somersault over the bench and weights.

Suddenly, I heard a loud crash and a scream. When I turned around, I saw Hillary sprawled out on the garage floor. The weight bench was lying on its side, and the two-hundred-pound barbell was lying over her tiny, fragile chest. Had the weights on the barbells been any smaller, her chest would have been crushed. Had the barbells fallen at a different angle across her body, she would have been killed.

Luckily, they fell in such a way that the heavily weighted piece of iron bridged her tiny chest but didn't touch it. I rushed over to her to see if she was alright and immediately lifted away the barbells.

I examined her ribs to see if any were broken. I put my ear to her chest to listen to her breathing. When I asked her if she was hurt, she said she wasn't. Then I did what any parent might do when a beloved child puts herself in mortal danger by doing a stupid act. I spanked her and warned her never to do it again.

Her tears began to flow. So did mine. She hurriedly ran to Nina, who was inside the house. It was a long time before Hillary came into my gym again.

Immediately, I regretted the spanking. It was unnecessary and stupid of me. It didn't occur to me when I spanked her that she had been frightened enough by that close call.

64. Peru - A Missionary Camp in the Jungle

In the fall of 1967, Nina and I and our close friends, Jan and Sandy Arak, planned an extensive six-week trip to South America. We had many memorable experiences on that trip, but one of the best was when we spent three days at a missionary camp in the Peruvian jungle on the Amazon River.

Boarding a small private plane out of Lima, Peru, we flew to a tiny landing field in the jungle along the Amazon. From there, we took a small flat-bottomed riverboat for a two-hour trip to our destination.

As we cruised down the river, protected from the hot tropical sun by a large awning, we heard the buzzing and humming of millions of insects and the screeching of monkeys as they swung from tree to tree.

Our boat veered into a narrow inlet and docked in front of a cluster of small cabins and lodges. This was the outpost of a group of Protestant missionaries who were there to educate and give health care to the natives who lived in this part of the rainforest.

We were escorted to our cabins, which were very primitive. The beds were built-in bunks swathed with mosquito netting. There was no running water, only a pitcher and basin. Toilets were in outhouses down a path about a hundred feet from the cabins. There was one shower for the whole camp. Water for the shower was accumulated rainwater that was stored in a tank on the roof and released into the shower by pulling on a chain.

After we were settled, our guide from the camp took us by a small canoe to the village of the local natives. They greeted us warmly. The men wore nothing but a loincloth. Their hair, which was cut into a short bob with bangs, was decorated with a wreath made from the colorful feathers of local birds. Women wore skirts made of grass but were naked from the waist up. They wore necklaces of bits of shell and feathers. The children wore nothing at all.

Their huts were made of local wood and bamboo. They had a thatched roof and rested on five-foot-long wooden stilts. The only entrance to the home was by a ladder. Inside was a single room about nine feet square. The only furniture was floor mats. On the walls hung several blowpipes.

Our guide led us to one side of the village to watch a blowpipe demonstration. The men were excellent hunters using these four-foot-long blowpipes made from the branches of special trees related to the nutmeg family. They used darts made from palm fronds that were tipped with poison, either curare from plants or secretions from poisonous frogs. We watched several of the tribesmen as they showed their skills by shooting at targets that hung from trees. Their accuracy was amazing. Our guide told us these hunters could kill a small monkey at ninety feet.

As we left, we saw the women preparing a huge boa constrictor for their evening meal. Back at the missionary camp, after a dinner that included a piece of dried monkey meat that tasted a little like jerky, our guide took us back onto the river.

We saw fierce black caimans, which are alligator-like creatures. We had been given flashlights, and as we shined our lights into the dark, we could see their eyes, glowing red, staring back at us.

The following morning, we were back on the Amazon again. Our guide pointed out the native children going to the missionary school by canoe. He showed us the voracious piranha fish that lurked below the surface of the river. As he dropped a large piece of meat into the water, there was a violent splashing and scrambling. The piranha devoured the meat in seconds.

When we returned to camp, one of the missionaries asked me to take a look at the eye of one of the native children. The eye was swollen, red, and protruding. A profusion of pus was draining from it. Luckily, the child could still see.

This was an infection left unattended that could be cured by the application of antibiotic drops. The missionary explained that, in case of illness, the natives would always go to their witch doctor at first and only come to the camp for treatment when healing did not occur. Sadly, there was nothing I could do.

The next day, we headed back up the river, back to the tiny landing strip, and flew back to civilization.

65. Italy and The Navy Blue Boots

As our children grew older, Nina and I were able to take them along with us when we traveled. One summer, when Alison was fourteen and Hillary was nine, we went as a family to Italy. We rented a black Mercedes sedan and hired an Italian guide who spoke excellent English, and together we took the whole tourist route: Rome, Venice, Capri, Pisa, and Milan.

At last, we arrived in Florence, that magnificent city of churches and museums; of the Duomo and the Uffizi; of Michelangelo's statue of David and Botticelli's painting of Venus; of the ancient family Medici; of the ancient bridge Ponte Vecchio; and of . . . oh, the *shoes!*

The first thing Alison and Hillary wanted to do in this city of artistic glory was to visit the famous leather school at the Basilica of Santa Croche. The school, over the years, had trained orphaned boys and girls in the skills of making leather goods and shoes. The products they made were of high fashion, excellent quality, and very, very expensive.

Neither girl found anything that pleased her among the vast assortment of shoes on display. Hillary wanted a pair that she could wear to school. But Alison had her heart set on a pair of navy-blue boots.

We left and continued our search among the dozens of fashionable shoe stores that surrounded the leather school. Hillary quickly found a pair of school shoes that pleased her and fit well, but not one pair of blue boots could Alison find.

Finally, as we were about to give up our search, Alison spotted, in a store window, a beautiful pair of navy-blue shiny boots with a two-inch heel.

We entered the store, relieved that the search had ended, and ordered the shoe salesman to bring the boots. Alison slipped her feet into the shiny blue boots. She pulled and tugged. She twisted and wiggled her feet. Finally, the boots were on. Too tight! Of course, there was not a larger size in the store. So we left and began our search again. No blue boots could be found.

Alison insisted that we go back to the store with the blue boots. "The boots fit fine," she said.

"They're way too small," I replied.

But Alison began to cry and complain that I was mean. And so back to the store we went.

Again, she squeezed her feet into the boots. "Don't worry," said the salesman. "They'll stretch after you wear them for a while."

I warned her never to buy shoes that don't fit when you first try them on, but Alison cried that she loved them and *needed* them. So I bought the boots and insisted that she wear them. Alison hobbled back to the hotel.

I strongly recommend that she wear the boots the next day even though Alison had now admitted they were very tight. She did, and while walking accidentally broke off one of the heels on the cobblestone-paved street. We all laughed as she limped along while we did our sightseeing, her gait going up and down like the horses on a merry-go-round. She begged me to let her wear her comfortable shoes, but I insisted that she wear the now cursed blue boots for the rest of the day.

In the evening, back in our room at the hotel, I let Alison take off the battered, uncomfortable boots. It took Alison, Nina, and I to get the boots off her very swollen feet.

"What do you think?" I asked her.

"I think I'll never again buy a pair of shoes that don't fit when I first try them on."

66. Benazir Bhutto (1953-2007)

On a Friday afternoon in 1987, a young Pakistani woman dressed in a beautiful yellow and blue silk sari came into my office. She was accompanied by four young women, also elegantly dressed in saris, whom she referred to as her attendants. All five women were laden with ornate gold jewelry that softly jingled as they moved. When I was finished with my previous patient, I escorted her into my private office for a consultation.

She told me her name was Benazir Bhutto and that she was from Karachi in Pakistan. She had come to me for a rhinoplasty. She had a rather large bump on the bridge of her nose that she wanted removed. She desired a straight nose, one that would allow her to breathe well.

I spoke with her, as I did with all of my patients, and learned that she would soon be married. She related that, as a wedding gift, her father had promised to give her one hundred saris from India, all of the highest quality. It was then that she mentioned her father had been prime minister of Pakistan (9th PM 1973-1977).

She spoke perfect English, and why not? She attended the finest schools in the United States, both Radcliffe and Harvard. Later, she completed her education at Oxford University in England.

She decided to go ahead with the surgery, which was done in the operating theater of my office under general anesthetic. She was very happy with the results. After several required post-op visits, she told me that she was going to return to her country.

After that, I never saw Benazir Bhutto again, and I was surprised when several years later I read in the local paper that she had been elected as the first woman prime minister of Pakistan.

Over the years, I followed her career in the newspapers and on television, including her second election as prime minister of the Peoples' Party of Pakistan and the charges made against her for corruption.

I heard of her exile in England and of her return to Pakistan to try to regain political power. Finally, I was saddened to hear of her assassination in 2007.

67. Tattoos, the Mayor, and Me

"I'm not going to remove any more tattoos for the Department of Social Services," I declared to the social worker.

I was speaking to this older gentleman, a social worker, who had in the past brought me many juvenile delinquents and older criminals to have me remove their offensive and pornographic tattoos.

I was speaking to him in my Sunset Boulevard office, where I'd been in practice for ten years. I knew it wasn't his fault. But I'd had it. For many years, I had been removing tattoos free of charge at the request of the department. Psychiatrists from Social Services thought that the removal of these tattoos would help in the rehabilitation of these offenders. When I was asked to help, I volunteered my services.

The removal of tattoos was an extensive procedure. It required a skin graft at times, and also the need for an anesthesiologist. Occasionally, a lot of bleeding occurred and a blood transfusion was needed. None of these patients had any insurance or the ability to pay. Not only did I provide my services, but I paid all expenses of these surgeries including the salaries of my assistants.

This fine day had been a long time coming. The reason I was so upset was that I never got a word of thanks from either a patient or the department. Not a card nor a letter of appreciation did I receive. The social worker left the office, admitting that he understood how I felt.

The convicts were usually brought to my office escorted by two armed policemen. They were in handcuffs and wearing bright orange prison garb. They entered the office by the back door so that my other surgical patients wouldn't see them.

All of the tattoos that I removed were truly bizarre and offensive.

Pictures of male and female genitalia were common, as were images of copulating couples. Profane language was inked all over some patients' bodies, as well as words of violence. Some of my patients could be violent, too. One threatened to come and kill me if he didn't like the results.

Two months later, I received a package from the city of Los Angeles. It contained a plaque of appreciation from Mayor Sam Yorty thanking me for my services.

68. Archbishop Sheen

In February 1969, I saw a notice in the American Medical Journal that the American Cancer Society was offering a fellowship in head and neck cancer surgery at Georgetown University in Washington, DC The applicant had to be board certified in plastic and reconstructive surgery. The fellow selected would receive a stipend of $2,500. This was the only fellowship offered by Georgetown in plastic surgery at this time.

The medical school at Georgetown, in conjunction with the National Institute of Health in Bethesda, Maryland, was noted for its expertise in the treatment of cancer of the head and neck. I thought this would be an excellent opportunity to hone my skills. So I applied for and was awarded the fellowship.

The fellowship was to last one month, so I had to make arrangements both in my office and at home for my absence. Nina wanted to come with me, and I looked forward to her company.

When we arrived at Georgetown, we were escorted to a lovely apartment on the campus, which was to be our home for the next month. It was within walking distance of the hospital.

In the evenings, after a day in surgery, I would often go to nearby Catholic University, where lectures were held in the library auditorium on religious subjects. One evening, as I was listening to a lecture, a priest sat down in the empty seat beside me.

He introduced himself as Fulton J. Sheen. As I looked into his handsome face, I immediately recognized him as the great Catholic communicator and television star who captivated millions of viewers every Sunday evening, Archbishop Fulton J. Sheen.

During intermission, although he was deluged by well-wishers and admirers, we had a chance to chat, and he asked me about my fellowship. He seemed interested and invited me to join him for a snack after the lecture. He took me to a restaurant, where we had pie and coffee. We talked about many things, but he was most interested in my boxing career. He said that he loved to box and often worked out at the Georgetown University gym. He suggested that we go a few rounds.

About a week later, Archbishop Sheen and I met at the gym. I was surprised to see how fit he was. He was in his early seventies (seventy-four, to be exact) yet had the muscular build of a much younger man.

I watched him as he hit the speed bag in perfect rhythm. He invited me to climb into the ring, and we began to spar. We were both wearing sixteen-ounce gloves so that no one could get really hurt.

In the third round, he walked into my right hook, which hit him squarely in the right eye. As the round continued, I noticed that his eye was beginning to bruise. I stopped the fight and applied an ice bag. Although he said it was nothing, I felt terrible about it. He told me that his makeup man could cover the bruise for his next TV show.

The next time I saw Fulton (for now we were on a first-name basis) was when I invited him out to dinner. I chose a fine restaurant with music and dancing in Georgetown. Nina was excited to join us. Bishop Sheen was a lot of fun to be with. He was an excellent conversationalist, could tell a good joke, and was a fine dancer.

When the band at the restaurant played "The Charleston," he grabbed Nina and whirled her around the dance floor. Later, when I complimented him on his dancing, he smiled and replied, "Well, I wasn't always a priest."

We saw each other a few more times, but then it was time for my fellowship to end and for us to go back to California.

One of the times that we were together, I told Father Sheen that sometime in the future I would like to spend some time in Calcutta, India, with Mother Theresa.

He said that when I was ready, he would be glad to make the arrangements. He then asked me to do him a favor, which was to deliver an envelope to Mother Teresa when I saw her. (This, I eventually did.)

We met one last time to say goodbye. As he wished me good luck and good health, he handed me a large manila envelope sealed in wax with his personal seal to be given to Mother Theresa.

Although I was dying to open this envelope, I never did.

69. India's Saint

Mother Teresa was the founder of the Missionaries of Charity, a Catholic order that established hospitals, clinics, orphanages, and soup kitchens around the world. She is most well known for her hospital and clinics in India, where patients with leprosy, yaws, malaria, AIDS, and other diseases were treated.

For a long time, I thought it would be interesting to work with Mother Teresa in Calcutta. The year before, in 1969, I had been with Archbishop Fulton Sheen in Washington, DC He knew of my desire and offered to arrange a preceptorship for one month when I was ready to go.

I still had his personal letter to Mother Teresa sealed with wax. About a year later, I'd telephoned Bishop Sheen at Catholic University and told him I was ready to go to India. Soon, I received a letter from Calcutta confirming my appointment.

In March of 1970, I flew on Air India out of New York to Bombay. The flight was no pleasure. The food was bad, the toilets overflowed into the cabin, and the weather was rough. At Bombay, I transferred to Indian Air for a pleasant flight to Calcutta.

From the airport, I took a taxi to "Mother Teresa's hospital." The driver knew the way without any directions.

I was greeted at the hospital by a nun wearing a white sari with a blue stripe around the border. She told me that I would meet Mother Teresa at dinner and then led me to my room. The room was austere with no furniture except a bed with a cross hanging over it, a desk with a lamp, and a chair.

Before we sat down for dinner, I was introduced to the staff and then to Mother Teresa herself. She was a tiny lady, not even five feet tall. She stood with her shoulders slightly stooped as if she had the weight of the world upon them. She had an olive complexion, and her skin showed many years of wear. She was deeply wrinkled. Even her wrinkles had wrinkles. But when she smiled, her brown eyes sparkled and radiated kindness. I just could sense she had a great sense of humor.

It was then that I handed her the letter from Archbishop Sheen. She thanked me and said that she was expecting it.

Suddenly, dinner was interrupted by the loud ringing of a bell. An ambulance had arrived with an emergency. One of our staff physicians, Dr. Percy Rolland from England, had been terribly injured.

He'd been on a train returning from a polo match. It was hot and humid with no air conditioning on the train. He opened the window, resting his arm on the sill. He was wearing his gold Rolex watch. The train was slowing as it pulled into the station, and an Indian beggar with an ax in his hand ran up to the train. He grabbed the doctor's arm and chopped his hand off at the wrist to get the watch.

We rushed into the operating room closely following Dr. Rolland. Someone had actually had the presence of mind and remembered to bring along the hand, but tragically it could not be reattached. We didn't have the proper equipment.

I was able to stop the bleeding and I prepared a skin flap to cover the wound. Once stabilized, he returned to England.

I was kept busy at the hospital. I treated many burns on children. Cooking was done over an open fire, and often a sari would catch fire as a child ran by. I also repaired children with harelips and cleft palates.

There was a problem with obesity. The people ate food that was highly caloric but low in food value. As a result, diabetes was rampant, as were problems with gallbladders. I did many amputations of fingers and toes on patients who'd lost circulation due to Hansen's disease, which is leprosy. All of the patients were poor.

The average worker earned forty-five cents a day. Everyone who was hospitalized needed to provide a caretaker, who was usually a family member. The caretaker would bring food and cook meals for the patient.

They would wash clothes and bed linens. They would bathe the patient and do whatever was needed to help the house medical staff.

There was little privacy in the wards of the main hospital. Beds were on tiered platforms in one large room, like an amphitheater. The nursing care was excellent, but painfully, there was always a shortage of drugs.

On the other hand, once the local team learned of my specialty, some of the nurses wanted to have cosmetic procedures like breast augmentation or liposuction. However, this type of surgery was taboo at this hospital.

When it was time to leave, Mother Teresa gave me a small party. We had cookies and tea. The whole staff was there. I said my goodbyes to everyone, then I stealthily walked up behind Mother Teresa and tapped her on her behind.

"Goodbye, Big Mama," I said loudly.

The whole room went deadly silent.

She slowly turned toward me with a big smile and, pointing her finger at me, said, "You're a bad boy."

70. The Party of the Century

In the early part of the 1970s, Mohammad Reza Pahlavi, the Shah of Iran, decided to give a big, big party. It was to celebrate the 2,500th anniversary of the founding of the Persian Empire by Cyrus the Great and the founding of the Imperial State of Iran.

He would invite royalty and heads of state and celebrities from all over the world. He would hold the party in the ancient city of Persepolis, which was the capital of Cyrus the Great.

The Shah would provide feasts catered by the finest chefs in the world and wines from the best vineyards in France. He would use the finest porcelain dinnerware, crystal glassware, and the best table linens available. He would erect an elaborate tent city to house the more than six hundred guests that he planned to invite. Cost was not important. Everything had to be the best. This fabulous celebration was to be held from October 12 to 16, 1971.

In the winter of 1970, I received a letter from a friend and colleague, Dr. Thomas Rees. Dr. Rees was chairman of the plastic surgery department at the Manhattan Eye, Ear, and Throat Hospital in New York City and one of the most prominent physicians in his field. He had been invited by the Shah of Iran to come to the big celebration.

In addition, he wanted Dr. Rees to come a little early to do some cosmetic procedures on the queen's friends, wives of diplomats and generals, or any lady of the queen's court who wanted a little "freshening up" before the big event.

In the letter, Tom Rees invited me to join him in Iran. I was president of the American Breast Society, and my expertise would be needed for any breast surgery that might be required.

At the end of September 1971, we, along with three other plastic surgeons who were experts in their field, boarded a Pan Am flight as first-class passengers out of New York to Tehran. Our fares were paid by the Shah.

When we landed at the Tehran airport, we were greeted by a general of the Iranian Air Force, who ushered us through customs before all of the other passengers. We were escorted to red Mercedes-Benz limousines and whisked away to the palace of the Shah. There, the five of us were led to a dining room for lunch. It was an elaborately decorated place with large crystal chandeliers and chairs upholstered in a golden silk fabric.

After lunch, we were shown to our rooms, where our luggage had been brought and unpacked. Each room was furnished with the most modern electronic equipment of the day: televisions, phones on which you could call home, and soft oriental-sounding music that was piped in.

There was a call cord available to summon servants if you needed anything. There was a big, soft feather bed in the room and a comfortable sofa to lounge on. Each room had a private marble bathroom with a window looking out onto a lovely garden below. Multicolored flowers in porcelain vases were placed here and there. Soaps, colognes, and shaving needs were there for our convenience.

The five of us were then taken to a different part of the palace to inspect the surgeries. There were two large, modern surgical theaters with a ten-bed recovery room. They were impressive. They contained all of the modern equipment that would be needed in case of an emergency.

All of the instruments that a plastic surgeon might need were provided in duplicate. They were of the finest quality. There was even a large supply of silicone breast implants of all sizes and shapes, as well as chin and cheek implants.

It had been a long day. We retired early after dinner. We had been treated like royalty.

The next day, I was awakened at 6:00 a.m. I had before me a sumptuous breakfast of assorted fruits and sweet rolls and black Persian coffee, which was brought in by a palace servant. The servant stood aside as I finished my breakfast and then assisted me with my shower. He then laid out my green surgical scrubs and my long, white lab coat to wear.

A nurse, who spoke fluent English, came to my room and escorted me to an examination room. She would be with me while I was with patients to help translate if needed. She also would be scrubbing in with me during surgery.

My first patient was a thirteen-year-old girl, the daughter of an air force general, who was accompanied by her mother. She had a very large mass in her left breast, which had been growing since she was ten. It was now the size of a grapefruit and greatly outsized by her right breast. Because of the girl's medical history, I knew that the mass was a fibro-adenoma, a growth that looked worse than it was. It was not cancerous nor life-threatening. The surgery was scheduled for two days later.

During this surgery, I removed a four-pound smooth tumor, which was easily excised. With the removal of the tumor, there was excess skin on the left breast, which I had to remove. I then equalized the size of both breasts by using saline implants, the implant on the right breast being a little larger than the one on the left. Both parents and the girl were delighted with the results.

In the evening after the first day of surgery, all of us doctors dressed for dinner and were escorted to a large dining room in the palace. It was there that we were introduced to the Shah, Reza Pahlavi, and his wife, Empress Farah.

We were seated at the table when they entered, led by his chamberlain. We all stood as the chamberlain announced His Majesty's name. The Shah thanked us for coming and said to let him know if we needed anything. He spoke perfect English, and his manner was very warm and friendly. He was elegantly dressed in a uniform with many medals. Empress Farah was an extremely beautiful woman with a lovely and welcoming smile.

One by one, we doctors approached the Shah to shake his hand as we told him who we were and where we were from. We bowed slightly as we met the Empress but did not touch her. They both left the room after the introductions.

After dinner, we were taken to a nearby reception room where a lively party was going on. The room was filled with military officers, mostly air force generals and their ladies. The women were introduced as "girlfriends." They were all beautifully dressed, wearing opulent jewelry, and were extremely attractive. The women seemed to be of many different nationalities, and you could hear many foreign languages spoken.

A joyous and romantic atmosphere permeated the place, with music from a large orchestra playing, wine and spirits flowing freely, and small delicious hors d'oeuvres passed among the happy guests. We later learned that these parties went on almost every night and that the women were available to us if we wished.

I was the only plastic surgeon in our group doing breast surgery. Most of my surgeries were augmentations, which enlarged the breast by using saline implants. I also corrected ptotic breasts, which were flat and hanging. In those, I had to remove skin before placing the implants. Only a few of my patients wanted their breasts made smaller.

I did a total of twenty-five surgeries while in Iran and happily, there were no complaints. In all of the surgeries I performed, there were Iranian plastic surgeons, board certified, who assisted me. They were there to learn the latest techniques in these types of procedures. All surgeries were done under general anesthetics.

Although I personally accepted no fees for the operations I performed, I pre-arranged that a donation of $125,000 be made to the American Breast Society for their philanthropic work in Africa.

Time passed quickly in Teheran. Besides surgery, we did a lot of sightseeing escorted by some air force generals. Soon, it was time for the grand anniversary celebration.

71. Eddie Nash

From time to time in my practice, I would meet a patient I found interesting and with whom I would later develop a personal relationship. One of these patients was Eddie Nash, also known as Adel Gharib Nasrallah. He came into the office for the removal of a small growth on his face, which I removed on his first visit.

It was a pleasant coincidence the next time I saw Eddie. I had booked a reservation for my daughter Hillary's sweet sixteen party at a restaurant on Hollywood Boulevard called The Seven Seas. This restaurant was very well known with very hard-to-get seats, because it was right across from the TCL Chinese Theatre at 6904 Hollywood Blvd.

I wanted a place that served lunch and had entertainment. This place offered, along with lunch and party balloons and streamers, a Hawaiian revue with music, hula dancers, and Polynesian music.

At the end of the show, Eddie came over to the table. I had no idea he owned the place. He was laughing and smiling while insisting that it was his pleasure to have me and my family there. Then he tore up the check.

Not long afterward, Eddie came to my office again, this time to have his nose reconstructed. He had breathing problems due to his habit of sniffing cocaine, which I was able to relieve.

Over time, he began to tell me of his history. It seemed he wanted to tell me all. Adel Nasrallah (AKA Eddie) was born in British Palestine to wealthy parents. It's said that they owned forty-seven hotels in and around Ramallah.

Eddie fled to the United States in the 1950s with his brother after Israel became a state in 1948 and the Israeli government confiscated his parents' land. He joined the United States Army and, having served a year, he was able to become a citizen. Eddie moved to Los Angeles and began buying real estate in Hollywood. He eventually became the owner of many buildings along the boulevard, and the proprietor of eighteen nightclubs—just to mention a few: W. Hollywood's P.J.'s Club/Starwood, Hollywood's the Soul'd Out Club, the Disco Odyssey, the Paradise Ballroom, The Seven Seas, Ali Baba's, and the strip club The Kit Kat.

Clearly, Eddie was an astute businessman—but had a checkered reputation. He was accused of being a drug dealer and of masterminding the gruesome "Wonderland Murders" that took place in the Hollywood Hills in 1981.

He denied all charges against him and, after a long and notorious trial, was acquitted. A few years later, the government went after him again, and he was arrested and charged with possession and sales of $1 million of narcotics. He was imprisoned for a term of three years and was forced to shake his substance dependence "cold turkey."

Eddie Nash and I eventually became good friends, and I found him to be a kind and generous man. He was married, had two boys, and was a loving husband and father. His manner was gentlemanly. We sometimes had lunch or dinner together. We once traveled together, cruising the Galapagos Islands, marveling at the exotic land animals, birds, and sea creatures there.

My good friend Eddie passed away in 2014 of a heart attack at the age of eighty-five. No matter his reputation, he was a devout Catholic and was buried with a solemn religious ceremony. I miss him.

72. We Gon' to Jamaica, Man!

Christmas break from school had arrived, and it was time for our yearly family vacation. Nina and I had promised the girls, now sixteen and eleven, that we would go to Jamaica, a destination suggested by one of my patients.

There, we could enjoy swimming and water sports, experience the reggae music and dance of the Jamaican culture, and do enough sightseeing to satisfy my curiosity and hunger for foreign places and people.

We arrived at our destination, the Sign Inn Great House in Montego Bay, only to find out that Alison's luggage had not arrived. After checking with American Airlines, we were told that it would be four days before her clothes could be redelivered. The airline offered one hundred dollars to buy replacement clothes, but Alison, not seeing anything to her fancy in the hotel store, opted to dress in the hotel's bedsheets until her suitcases were returned.

The hotel offered a bus tour of the island, and we eagerly took advantage of the free excursion. One of the stops was at Nonsuch Caves, a haven for thousands of bats. As we entered the cave, our feet squished through piles of guano and the odor was stifling. Our presence startled the bats, and hordes of them flew out of the cave, scaring the girls.

Another interesting stop was called Cockpit Country, a rugged area on the northern tip of Jamaica. The limestone karst topography was riddled with caves and sinkholes.

That evening at the hotel, we enjoyed dinner out on a terrace scented with roses and gardenias. A reggae band and singer entertained us. Nina and I let the girls sample a banana daiquiri, which they loved but made them very sleepy. Happily, we put them to bed early.

The hotel had a large stable, and one morning, I decided to go for a ride. I approached the stable master, a tall, muscular Jamaican, who asked me in his lilting native dialect how well I could ride. I replied that I was an excellent rider, and he led me to a huge chestnut-colored spirited stallion.

Off the two of us rode into the forested highlands. All went well until the stable master's horse, sensing a rattlesnake's nest, stopped abruptly. My horse, frightened, reared up. Over the back of the saddle I fell, landing on my back. Luckily, I was unhurt.

Unexpectedly, Alison's luggage arrived in three days instead of four, and so our family was able to take advantage of the lovely Jamaican beaches and the hotel pool.

One day, we rented a car and decided to do some exploration on our own. The car was a British make, a convertible. We had the top down and were enjoying the pleasant weather. We drove to the historic Rose Hall, a large house and estate also in Montego Bay on Cinnamon Hill.

The mansion was built in 1734 by Edward Barrett, an ancestor of the famous English poet Elizabeth Barrett-Browning. In the early 1970s, the famous singer Johnny Cash purchased it. After the death of the Cash family, it was reacquired by the scions of the Rollins family in 2012. The Cash family and island lore recount numerous sightings and haunted experiences in Rose Hall. The legend of Annie Palmer, referred to by her slaves as the "white witch" of Rose Hall, is told to this day.

Hauntingly, as we left Rose Hall, a sudden tropical downpour exploded. The carburetor of the car flooded, and the car stalled. I dried it off with a towel. The car started. In a few miles, the carburetor flooded again. Again, the car stalled, and again, I dried off the carburetor. This was no way to spend a vacation!

We finally made it back to the hotel, where we returned the car. By that time, of course, the storm was over. We opted to spend the rest of the day at the pool.

We all loved this trip to Jamaica—the sightseeing, the azure waters, the wonderful music, and the friendly natives. But, believe it or not, the thing that my girls remember most fondly was when Alison lost her luggage and ran around wrapped in a bedsheet.

73. Preceptorship

By 1972, my practice had grown so large that I needed a partner or a preceptor to assist me in handling the volume of patients. I considered a partnership, but I wasn't ready to hand over part of my practice to someone else.

A preceptorship is a process of teaching an experienced doctor another field of medicine or surgery. In my case, of course, the field would be plastic, cosmetic, and reconstructive surgery. To have this program, I had to submit my curriculum vitae, along with a record of the number and types of surgeries I had performed in the previous five years. I submitted these records to the American Board of Plastic and Reconstructive Surgery. I was approved by the board to have two fellows each year. The preceptorship would last for two years.

My office on Sunset Boulevard was well equipped. I had two surgical theaters and a two-bed recovery room. I had as much lifesaving and resuscitation equipment as is required in a hospital. A full-time anesthesiologist was always present during operations. The office also had three treatment rooms, a photography room, a supply room, my own private office, a scheduling room, and a very large reception room with a business office.

When I was approved for the program, I put an ad in the Plastic and Reconstructive Journal announcing the availability of my preceptorship. To my surprise, I got fifty-two applicants.

I was looking for a physician, the one most experienced in one of the surgical specialties such as general surgery, maxillofacial surgery, EENT, obstetrics and gynecological surgery, and dermatological surgery. He had to have a pleasant personality and meet patients well. I wanted someone with an inquisitive nature. He had to dress appropriately and be well groomed. Any fellow that I might choose had to be able to secure hospital privileges locally.

I interviewed all the applicants and was most impressed by Dr. Richard Caleel, who was already chief of surgery at a Chicago medical school and had his own private practice in that city. He met all my requirements and, in addition, was a wonderful speaker with a big booming voice. He started as my first fellow in the fall of 1972. He also was an amazing polo horseman.

My second fellow was a young maxillofacial surgeon from Kansas, Dr. John Tanner, who received both medical and dental degrees from Northwestern University.

For the first two months, I would have my fellows observe a surgical procedure. Their participation would be minor. We would discuss my method of surgery, and if any variations were suitable or necessary.

I frequently quipped, "There's more than one way to skin a cat."

As time went on, I gave them more privileges in the operating room, but never more than I thought they could handle. The well-being of the patient was always primary, and my responsibility. I would never permit the fellows to operate without my presence or do a complete surgery by themselves.

My fellows proved to be especially helpful in post-operative care. They could change dressings and check the progress of a patient's healing without my direct supervision. This would allow me more time with new patients.

Toward the end of the training program, if a fellow had acquired his own patient, I would permit him to do the whole surgery, but only with me in the room. All of my fellows had to carry their own malpractice insurance, but none of them were ever sued.

Over the coming decades, I had trained thirty fellows in cosmetic surgery. All of them had to take a certification examination to practice this specialty and all of them passed. I am very proud of them.

74. The Motorcycle Accident

"No horseback riding today," said the chief wrangler of the Double U Ranch. "The ground will be too slippery and unstable for the horses."

There had been a three-day downpour in the usually arid Sonora Desert in Arizona. I was looking forward to a horseback ride to Seven Falls, a remarkable and scenic waterfall in the Santa Catalina Mountains. A group of eight of us put together this adventure trip.

For the past four years, from 1970 to 1974, I had taken Nina and our girls to this dude ranch in Arizona during the kids' Christmas break from school. My family loved coming here for all the fun and activities. There was square dancing, movies, card playing, and gambling in the evenings. In the daytime, there were all sorts of sports activities and, of course, my favorite, horseback riding.

That morning, one of the fellows suggested that since we couldn't ride horses to get to Seven Falls, we should rent dirt bikes. We all agreed that this was a great idea and headed to the rental shop on Speedway Blvd. The shop only had six dirt bikes available, but there was also one street bike, a Harley-Davidson. The Harley was twice the weight of the dirt bikes and required a more skilled rider.

I was the most experienced, having owned three motorcycles in the past, and so I volunteered to ride it. One disappointed friend had to return to the Double U Ranch.

Off we went, with me leading the pack, down Speedway Blvd. toward the desert and the Santa Catalina Mountains. The desert was beautiful. The cacti and desert flowers were in full bloom, fed by the rain of the past three days. The colors of the blooms—red, green, purple, and yellow—were vivid against the soft brown of the moist desert sand. The air was sweetly scented by this profusion of growth.

Higher and higher, the five-foot-wide pathway led us up the mountain toward the falls. As we climbed, we could see the desert floor about eighty feet below us. Suddenly, I felt the soil under the heavy weight of the Harley begin to slip. I began to panic as the earth collapsed and the bike slid out of my control down the side of the mountain. Down I fell, and as I descended, the bike twisted and turned, throwing me off the seat and, with the footrest bar, goring me in my left groin like an angry bull.

My fall was stopped by a protruding ledge on the side of the mountain about forty feet above the valley floor. Luckily, the bike landed beside me. There I lay on the ledge, not unconscious but bleeding heavily from the gash in my left upper leg.

I knew I needed a tourniquet to stop the bleeding. I yelled for help as I saw my friends, who had stopped when they saw me fall. One of my friends, Bert Jacobs, remounted his dirt bike and sped back to the highway, where he was able to flag down a truck with a radio transmitter. He called the fire department, which dispatched a rescue squad of six men.

Another one of the riders, Kenny Tucker, carefully climbed down the rugged terrain to the ledge where I was lying. He looked under my torn denims at the wound and fainted. He revived in a minute and apologized.

I directed him to tear the sleeve off his shirt to be used as a tourniquet. I had him tie the sleeve around my left leg above the wound and apply pressure until the blood stopped. I instructed him to release the pressure every twenty minutes and then reapply it until the blood stopped again.

The rescue team arrived an hour later. The rescue was complicated. The truck had to use the valley floor as its base. The firemen had to set up a series of pulleys and posts to send up a stretcher for me and then lower me back to the ground.

I was taken to an emergency hospital in Tucson. There, under local anesthetic because I wanted to see what the surgeon was doing, I was reassembled. It took one hundred and twenty stitches to repair the damage.

After the surgery, I was driven back to the Double U Ranch, where I recuperated for a week. I had paid for a two-week vacation and I was darned if I was going to waste the money. Nina and the girls were very sympathetic, and they managed to enjoy their vacation.

Our dirt bike ride and my accident were the talk of the ranch for a while. The consensus was that we were a bunch of wild men trying to be kids. I never rode a motorcycle again or even missed it.

75. Our Rumble in the Jungle

On a trip to South Africa in 1980, Nina and I wanted to visit the diamond mines, for which the region is famous. We went on a tour with about fourteen other travelers. First, we visited the Baken Diamond Mine located along the lower Orange River. We then continued south along the Orange. That was about when a huge rainstorm developed, and almost instantly the roads became impassable.

We were unable to reach the hotel that was booked for our trip. The closest place to stay was a local hotel-bar. Our guide thought this was the best place for the night because of the fierceness of the storm. The structure was a three-story dilapidated wooden building. As we drove up, we could hear loud music playing African rhythms.

It was Saturday night, and this was the night for the mine workers to "howl" because there was no work the next day. Given the conical shape of the strip mines, water was a constant hazard.

Within minutes of our arrival, it became clear this "hotel" was actually a whorehouse with entertainment, singing, music, and dancing downstairs. Working girls were there for the taking. These girls were young and very attractive and were dancing provocatively.

As I started to check in, I noticed that a lot of the men were drunk and falling over each other. I realized what kind of place we were in and asked our tour guide if there wasn't a better place to stay. He replied that this was the only available place for miles and that the bus could go no farther in the deep mud.

We were escorted to our room, which was on the second floor. It was a drab, unattractive place lit by a single light bulb screwed into the ceiling. Besides a rumpled bed, there was a cigarette-scarred wooden table and a wooden chair. There was no bathroom or running water in the room. Facilities were outside of the hotel near a garbage heap.

Our luggage remained in the bus guarded by the driver, who locked himself inside for safety. As much as we hated the room, Nina and I were tired and went to bed still dressed in our clothes.

Bang! Bang! There began loud knocking at the door. We heard drunken voices shouting and yelling.

I shouted back through the door, "You've got the wrong room. Go ask the manager where your room is."

Unfortunately, the African miners, the ones who were at the door, spoke only Swahili and didn't understand a word of English. The wooden door to the room was weak and unstable, and, after the pounding, came off its hinges and fell to the floor. Into the room came three angry, burly men. They came at me with fists swinging and started to attack.

Nina, terrified, huddled in the bed, the blankets pulled up to her chin. She screamed for me to do something. I grabbed the wooden chair and, by smashing it on the floor, broke off one of the legs.

As one of the miners took another swing at me, I hit him on the forehead with the leg, causing a four-inch vertical laceration. Blood spurted from the wound and ran onto his face. The shock of the encounter quickly sobered the intruders, and the fighting suddenly halted.

The hotel manager and our tour guide, hearing the ruckus, came running. I explained to them what had happened. I acknowledged that it was all a misunderstanding. I offered my services as a plastic surgeon to stop the bleeding and repair the wound. After translating my offer to the miner, the manager led us all to his office.

There, he cleared off his desk. The miner lay down, and I applied pressure to stop the bleeding. Then I taped the laceration together and reassured him that he would heal in about a week with only a small scar.

By morning, the rain had stopped. Happy to leave, we boarded our bus and sped off to the next diamond mine.

76. Microsurgery at Johns Hopkins

It was early in November of 1980 when I read in a medical journal about an interesting course would be offered at Johns Hopkins University on the topic of microsurgery.

The course was to last one week. To qualify, you had to be board certified in general surgery and be in a teaching position at a medical school. I qualified in both criteria and was excited at the prospect of learning the techniques of a discipline that was new to me.

I called my friend and former fellow, Dr. Richard Caleel, who was now chief of surgery at the Midwestern Medical School to see if he would be interested in taking the course with me. He was excited at the prospect of joining me, and we decided to bring our wives, Nina and Annette. While Richard and I were in class, the ladies could explore the fascinating and historical areas of Washington, DC, and Baltimore.

Johns Hopkins University School of Medicine is located in a very poor neighborhood of Baltimore. There is a very high crime rate in the area of the school. Because of this, nurses often requested that school guards accompany them to their cars in the parking lot for fear of being robbed or raped.

The course was given in the neurosurgical department of Johns Hopkins Hospital on the fourth floor. The class was often interrupted by the sound of emergency helicopters landing on the roof one floor above us.

The course was intensive. There were only two students, Dr. Caleel and me. There was one teacher, Dr. Herman Shor, who was a veterinarian. Each day, we were given a fresh rat, one that had not been operated on before. Each day, Dr. Shor presented several problems that we would have to correct surgically—for example: connect a vein to an artery, connect one artery to two veins, connect three veins to one artery, or connect two arteries to a vein and an organ.

The most important thing in doing these procedures was that the mouse survive. We used high-powered glasses during the operations along with special small, fine microsurgical instruments.

Richard Caleel was a fast operator. I was much slower in performing the procedures than he. He would tease me about my lack of speed. I didn't care as long as my mouse was still alive at the end.

During the day, while we were busy learning the ins and outs of microsurgery, our wives saw such sights as Fort McHenry of "Star Spangled Banner" fame in Baltimore Harbor and the newly refurbished aquarium. They toured the nearby naval academy at Annapolis and explored the many local antique shops. In the evenings, the four of us would go out to dinner at some highly recommended gourmet restaurant.

Friday was the last day of class and the day of our final exam. We were each given a rat. We had to graft two arteries to a renal artery and one vein to a renal vein. Although soft music was playing in the background of the operating lab, we surgeons were unusually quiet, fully concentrating on our "patients." We could feel the tension in the air. Richard, working in his quick, smooth, professional manner, finished his surgery a full half hour before me.

When I was almost finished, he walked over to my table, patted me on the back, smiled, and said, "Let's go to lunch."

After lunch, on the way back to the surgical lab, Richard was still teasing me about my slow methodical technique. As we entered the lab, Dr. Shor greeted us at the door. He turned to Richard and said, "Dr. Caleel, I'm sorry to tell you but your rat has died."

I cautiously walked over to the operating table where my rat was still tied down. I was happy to see that he was slowly moving around. Richard Caleel and I learned a lot from our course in microsurgery. We both received certificates of completion. However, he never talked about his dead rat.

77. Passports to Freedom

While attending a bar mitzvah at Temple Beth Shalom in the San Fernando Valley, I was approached by a rabbi. He was a gentleman I had never met, yet somehow he'd heard that Nina and I were planning a trip to Russia and the Ukraine. He asked if I would be willing to carry some American passports with me to be delivered to a specific location in Moscow.

The year was 1986, and the Soviet Union was still in control of many countries in vast areas of Asia and Europe. There was persistent and noxious anti-Semitism in Soviet Russia and the Ukraine. Many Jews wanted to immigrate to the United States, Israel, and the West.

I agreed to carry twenty-five American passports, unnamed, with me to the Soviet Union. The rabbi directed me to go to a specific tailor in North Hollywood, who would make me a custom-made blue serge jacket with enough hidden pockets to accommodate the passports.

This I did, and I enclosed a one-hundred-dollar bill into each passport that the tailor provided. The tailor carefully sewed the passports into the coat, then he gave me a note, written in Russian, with directions as to whom and where the passports should be delivered.

I chose not to tell Nina what I was up to, and our flight to Moscow was uneventful. I had been searched before boarding, but the jacket had been packed away into my suitcase. We went through Soviet customs without a problem and took a taxi to our hotel.

The following morning after breakfast, I put on the blue serge coat and had the doorman hail a cab. I showed the doorman the note with the directions that the tailor had given me. The doorman gave these directions to the driver of the cab.

I was surprised when the cab driver pulled up in front of an old government building. When he told me that this was the headquarters of the police, I began to feel very nervous. I summoned up my courage, went inside, and showed the note to a receptionist. He directed me to an office on the second floor, room number 5.

I knocked at the door, and it was opened by a burly, cigar-smoking Russian with a holster and gun slung over his left shoulder.

I showed him the note, and he grabbed my arm and pulled me up a flight of stairs to a bathroom with lockers in it. He patted down my jacket and then indicated for me to take it off. Again, he patted down the jacket, making sure that all twenty-five passports were there. Satisfied, he took the jacket, placed it in one of the lockers, and handed me another jacket, which was an exact duplicate but without the passports.

We never spoke a word to each other, but as I put on the blue serge jacket that he had given me and was ready to leave, he grabbed my hand and in broken, Russian-accented English, he said, "Thank you."

78. Komodo Island

Around Christmas in 1989, while on a trip to Indonesia, Nina and I decided to take a side trip to the mysterious and infrequently visited island of Komodo. I had heard about the monstrous and vicious lizards that inhabited this place and made up my mind to see these creatures in their natural environment.

We, along with fourteen other doctors, took an excursion boat leaving from Jakarta for a two-hour trip to the isolated island. There was no dock by which the boat could be anchored, and so from the depth of four feet, we waded ashore.

On the beach, I saw signs warning of the danger of attack by the Komodo dragons and prohibitions on exploring the island without a guard. We were met by our guard, a young Indonesian man carrying a high-powered rifle.

The island was mostly level and covered with long, heavy grass. There were a few trees scattered here and there. On the north side of the island were a few hills. This was where the guards and their families lived in a fortified compound. All supplies for living had to be brought in by boat.

As we walked along a dirt trail, our guard explained that the trail was made by the body and tail of the dragon as it went in search of prey. Along the way, we saw a memorial, like a small tombstone, to a Dutch explorer who had been attacked and eaten by a Komodo dragon in 1980.

Earlier in the morning, a group of guards had shot a wild deer. They dragged the deer along the ground, allowing its blood to seep into the earth and thereby spreading the scent for the monstrous lizards to follow. They hung the body of the deer on a ten-foot pole that stood at the bottom of a broad, fifteen-foot depression. This allowed visitors to safely view the dragons as they voraciously fed.

We saw a group of about eight dragons head toward the body of the deer. The creatures were about ten feet long. We watched as they slithered along the ground, moving their tails and heads from side to side and flicking their yellow tongues to better capture the scent.

We were told that these lizards can detect carrion from three to six miles away; that their saliva is poisonous, and one bite can kill you; that their saliva is also an anti-coagulant, and that they live to be about thirty years old. We learned that the female lays about thirty eggs in a self-dug megapode and that it takes about seven to eight months for the eggs to hatch.

We watched with fascination and disgust as the lizards devoured the deer. They climbed over one another, growling and snapping and even taking large chunks of flesh out of each other in their excitement. Before the feeding frenzy was over, we doctors were led by our guard back to our awaiting boat.

As I sailed back to Jakarta, I felt as though I had been transported, if only for a little while, back to the time of the dinosaurs.

79. My Most Expensive Phone Call

In December 1992, I decided to return to Indonesia. Indonesia is always hot and humid, even in the winter. Part of my trip included a cruise in the Straits of Sunda, and I was eager to pursue one of my favorite sports, scuba diving, which I would be able to do in the warm tropical waters.

The day before I left, a new patient came into my office. She was one of the chief reporters of the *National Enquirer*. She told me that she was getting married within a month and that she wanted to look her best.

She had heard about a new drug, Botox, which had just come onto the market, and wanted to know if it could get rid of her forehead wrinkles. I had never had any experience with the drug, but from what I'd read, Botox injections would certainly get rid of her forehead wrinkles.

She decided to go ahead with the injections, and before she left the office, she could see the results. Her forehead was smooth as a baby's. My patient was delighted.

After she left, I noticed that there was some Botox left in the bottle. I didn't want to waste it, so I injected my own forehead. The effect of the drug was immediate. I had no more lines in my forehead. Also, as the side-effect warning on the package stated, I could no longer raise my brows. I knew that this would be temporary, so I was not at all concerned.

The following day, I departed. Two days later, I boarded *The Indonesian Explorer*, which was docked in Jakarta. It was a small boat that accommodated about twenty-four travelers along with the crew. Even though it was small, the boat had all the facilities for fishing or scuba diving that any of the passengers might need.

As soon as we were able, a group of us enthusiastic scuba divers put on our breathing equipment and dove one hundred and fifty feet until we reached the bottom of the straits. The underwater scape was not disappointing. We encountered carp that were two feet long. There were red snappers and small sharks. Tiny, colorful tropical fish darted about, and jellyfish floated near the surface. Sea plants, too, were everywhere, some quite colorful.

We had been underwater for only forty minutes when a diver from the ship came down with a sign bearing my name. It read, "Dr. Koire, You have an emergency call. Come to the pilot's office immediately."

I ascended slowly to avoid the bends and was helped aboard by the crew. I went immediately to the pilot's office and was handed the phone. It was a shore-to-ship telephone call from my patient who had received the Botox injections three days before. My office staff had given her the number where I could be reached.

She was worried and upset. She couldn't raise her eyebrows. I had forgotten to tell her that there would a paralysis of the brow but that it would resolve in two to three months. Being assured that this was not a permanent problem, my patient became very chatty. She was sorry that she had bothered me and began to tell me about her wedding plans.

I, meanwhile, was looking at the clock on the wall of the pilot's office, counting the passing minutes of what I knew would be a very expensive call. The time included all of the minutes it took to fetch me from the bottom of the sea until I was finally able to get my patient off the phone.

I was not surprised when I opened my bill from the telephone company the following month. The cost of my little forgetfulness was $550.

80. Krakatoa

Flashing lights and volcanic extrusions were all about us when we landed by small inflatable zodiacs on the tiny volcanic island of Krakatoa.

As we approached, the ocean waters were warm and sometimes even hot from the flow of the lava cascading down from the mouth of the crater. Huge chunks of white pumice, some as big as a washing machine yet as light as a loaf of bread, floated on the dark-blue waters.

The air was so thick with smoke, ashy debris, and splinters of stone that it was impossible for me to wear my contact lenses because of the scratching it caused to my corneas. The distinctive smell of sulfur permeated the air.

I was among a small group of physicians and their families exploring by boat the many small Indonesian islands in the Straits of Sunda. We were in the company of an Indonesian volcanologist who was sent by the government to study the recent activity of the volcano.

This small volcano, called by the natives "child of Krakatoa," began to emerge in 1927 from the caldera of the original Krakatoa, which erupted in 1883. That eruption was so vast and loud that the sound could be heard three thousand miles away (the loudest sound in human history), and its explosion caused vast, destructive tsunamis.

Once on the island, the ground was so slippery that it was difficult to walk. The landscape was desolate. Any plant life there was charred and blackened. Giant clouds of black smoke billowed continuously from the volcano's mouth. I saw no animals, no birds.

We had been given box lunches so that we could picnic on the volcanic shore, but this was impossible because of the smoke and sediment in the air. And so, a bit disappointed, my fellow tourists and I boarded the small zodiacs, which took us back to our cruising ship.

In the dark of night, as I viewed Krakatoa from the deck of our ship, I could see the orange and red flames bursting from the cauldron like shooting stars.

Its reflection on the black, glassy waters lit up the Straits of Sunda like the lights of Broadway.

It was magnificent. It was Mother Nature's display. I had to see it!

81. The Attack of the Wild Baboon

Two of my greatest pleasures are traveling and visiting hospitals all over the world to see how medicine is practiced in foreign places. Happily, I could combine the two by taking tours designed for doctors that gave me continuing medical education credits and satisfied my desire to learn about other countries and cultures.

In the winter of 1993, I traveled to Tanzania and Kenya with a group of physicians from all over the United States. Our group met in Nairobi, Kenya, at the Nairobi Hilton Hotel, where on the following morning, about thirty-five of us, doctors and families, boarded a luxury air-conditioned bus to commence a fascinating and enlightening tour of the national parks of east Africa.

Kenya and Tanzania have an incredible variety of geological and geographical surprises. There are endless plains like the Great Rift Valley, which was formed by an earthquake in ancient times.

There are snow-covered mountains at the equator like Mount Kilimanjaro, where a glacier still stands. There are lakes and rivers that nourish a multitude of species, including the "big five": elephants, lions, buffalo, rhinos, and leopards. There are huge herds of zebras and gnus grazing on the grassy plains of the Serengeti, and groups of giraffes nibbling on the acacia trees in the Masai Mara. And birds; there are thousands upon thousands of them from the beautiful pink flamingos to the ever-ravenous vultures feasting on carrion left by carnivorous predators.

The attack occurred on December 30. It was lunchtime, and our tour bus had stopped on a bluff overlooking the Mara River, which forms part of the boundary between Kenya and Tanzania. The tour company had packed box lunches for our group, and we all looked forward to a picnic lunch overlooking a widening of the river swarming with more than one hundred crocodiles. This was a perfect spot for the crocodiles to snare a zebra or a wildebeest as it crossed the Mara.

I decided to have my lunch a little apart from the group. As I was finishing my lunch, I noticed a troop of about twenty-five baboons crossing the road some fifty yards from where we were sitting. After seeing the baboons, I thought to go back to the bus, but I wasn't ready to leave this ideal spot just yet. I pulled out from the lunch box the dessert, which was a juicy navel orange.

I held it up in the air, admiring its size, when I heard a chattering and shrieking. I looked up and saw a huge male baboon with grayish-brown fur rumbling, tumbling, and charging toward me.

He must have been the leader of the troop because the others had stayed behind and he was the largest of them all. He raced toward me on all fours with his tail held high in the air, slobbering and flashing his two large pointed canine teeth.

When he was almost upon me, I instinctively rolled onto my side in a fetal position with the orange still clutched in my hand. Then I felt him. It felt like a truck running over me as he snatched the orange from my hand and sped away into the trees, followed by his troop.

Then it was over. My heart was palpating rapidly and loudly. I felt scratches on my side and stomach, but other than that, I was alright. When I returned to the bus, some of the other doctors checked me over and decided that I would only need to take antibiotics to prevent any infection caused by the scratches. Luckily, I'd had a tetanus booster before I left on the trip.

Later in the day, as I mulled over my frightening experience of the afternoon, I thought, "What a great story to tell my grandkids."

82. St. Catherine's Monastery

In the winter of 1995, I traveled to Egypt with a group of college professors on a tour led by Dr. Leon Rosenstein from San Diego. Our two-week adventure was crammed with fascinating sights and experiences. We visited ancient Egyptian temples and pyramids, museums, and tombs. We sailed the Nile River to Alexandria and explored ancient Christian catacombs. We meandered the streets of Cairo where donkey-pulled carts mingled with automobiles, and we stayed in luxurious western-style hotels. One of the more interesting experiences we had was our journey to Saint Catherine's, a monastery in the mountains of the Sinai Desert.

The legend tells of Saint Catherine, a young girl from Alexandria who was tortured and beheaded because of her Christian faith. She was said to have been carried by angels to what is now Mount Saint Catherine, which is near Mount Sinai. There, three hundred years later, her bones were discovered by Christian monks. Later, the Byzantine Emperor Justinian I (527-565 CE) established the monastery in her honor.

We traveled by tour bus from Cairo through the Sinai Desert, passing oases of date palms, occasional hot springs, and beautiful but stark desert landscapes. Once in a while, we saw groups of Bedouins tending their sheep. We saw the Suez Canal with its cargo ships and the Red Sea, across which Moses led his people to freedom, but which is now a paradise for scuba divers. Finally, we arrived in the area of Saint Catherine's to spend the night at a small hotel at the foot of Mount Sinai.

Our accommodations there were spartan. The electricity had failed the night that we arrived so that there was neither light nor heat. Our dinner was cold. There was no hot water for showering or heat to warm the frigid desert night. But worst of all were the beds that were concrete slabs covered by itchy camel hair blankets.

Some of our fellow passengers opted to rise before dawn so that they could hike the crude trail to the top of Mount Sinai to see the beautiful sunrise. I decided not to go. I had seen many beautiful sunrises.

The following morning, our bus carried us up a narrow winding dirt road to the monastery. The monastery was surrounded by a high tan granite wall. The only thing we could see from the outside was the tall bell tower with its arched niches that was part of the ancient Greek Orthodox Church complex inside.

An old monk led our group through the massive wooden gates to a garden-filled interior. He led us to the "burning bush" where it's said God spoke to Moses, instructing him to free his people from Egyptian slavery. The bush (rubus sanctus) is tall and thriving now, more like a thickly leafed tree and protected by a high brown stone wall. The monk then took us to a basilica church. Inside, the walls were covered with magnificent icons. The faces of Christ, the Virgin Mary, and saints peered at us from across the millennia. In another church was the renowned library that contained hundreds of ancient manuscripts and some of the earliest printed books and bibles.

Next, he guided our group to a small building in the gardens of the monastery which lie outside its massive walls. It was the ossuary. Land for burial here is very scarce. When a monk dies, he is buried in a small cemetery next to the garden. Later, his bones are exhumed and placed in the ossuary.

It was unsettling to see the skulls and bones on display in such mountainous piles. It made one think of life and death, and of how insignificant we all are.

Having finished our visit to St. Catherine's, our group boarded the tour bus and headed back to Cairo. I will always treasure the memories of this ancient and holy place.

83. September 11, 2001

Every American of a certain age remembers where they were on September 11, 2001. It was a date of a great American tragedy. I was on vacation in the Dordogne region in the Southwest of France. After spending several days in Paris, on September 9, I boarded a high-speed train to Bordeaux, where I met my guide, Laurent. He knew the region well.

Seated comfortably in the back seat of Laurent's black limousine, I was driven through the lush wine country around Saint-Emilion. I explored this charming town, walking along its cobbled streets, seeing the ruined churches built by ancient kings, and lunching at a quaint café.

For another day, I continued my sightseeing: the museum of pre-history at Les Eyzies and the Font de Gaum cave, where I saw prehistoric paintings of wild horses. Then I was driven to the medieval town of Sarlat. I spent the night just outside the town at a lovely hotel that was part of a golf resort. The next day, Laurent was to drive me to the famous Lascaux caves.

That next day, however, was September 11, 2001. Laurent picked me up early in the morning. Later, he said that he was confused, that something terrible was happening in our country but that he didn't understand what it was. He had heard something about it on his car radio.

I didn't go back to my room to watch this "bad thing" that was happening but drove on to the Lascaux caves to see the magnificent prehistoric wall paintings. There are actually two caves. Lascaux I is the true prehistoric cave where only scientists and scholars are allowed entry. Tourists are taken to Lascaux II, a replica.

I was not disappointed. I saw paintings of horses, bison, deer, and bulls as they stampeded across the ceiling and walls. The details of these ancient animals, painted by some prehistoric artists, were true.

I remained unsettled the whole day. I was anxious to get back to the hotel to see what had happened at home. I turned on the TV and immediately saw the horror and devastation—the planes crashing into the twin towers, the black smoke pouring out of the buildings, the desperate people leaping out of the windows to their deaths. I saw the bravery of the first responders in their futile rush to save as many victims as they could, and the heartbreak of those families who had lost loved ones.

I watched these scenes of terror and destruction over and over and over.

I continued my journey the next day and was surprised at the sympathy shown by the French people. "Ah, you are American," they would say. "We are so sorry about what happened to your country."

In one of the small towns that we visited, there was a memorial service for the Americans who had died in that terrorist attack on September 11. I attended.

I returned to Paris. America had closed her doors. There could be no reentry, no incoming flights for a time. When the airline finally called and said I could now return to my homeland, I hurriedly packed and went to Charles de Gaulle Airport.

Instinctively, passengers looked around suspiciously at any Arab or Middle Eastern passenger, apprehensive that he might board the plane with us. Could he be a terrorist, too? How quickly had that massive terrorist attack of September 11, 2001, changed us!

EPILOGUE
By Bernie's Family

Bernie began to write these stories in the last few years of his life. If he had the time, he would have had many more stories to tell. He would have loved to have told you about an escapade he had as a teenager with his best buddy, Nathan. He would have described how they took Nathan's father's truck out for a joy ride, and how they were stopped by the police when they couldn't figure out how to put the truck into reverse gear.

He might have told you of the time that he dined at the home of a tribal chieftain in Papua, New Guinea, and how the chief's wife served a typical native feast wearing nothing but a tiny grass skirt.

Bernie might have explained to you how he and Nina found and bought their dream home in Pacific Palisades, California, the kind of house he thought, as a poor boy growing up in Philadelphia, existed only in movies. Having worked his way out of poverty and reached the pinnacle of his profession, he embraced success as a handsome, cool, self-assured, beautifully dressed, self-made man. He drove a classic Mercedes convertible, loved to listen to Frank Sinatra, was an accomplished dancer at social events, and could play the trumpet at parties.

And he would have had the opportunity to discuss his growing family about which he became so proud. He would have told sometimes hilarious stories about family adventures with his adult children and their children. Like other aspects of his life, Bernie threw himself into his role as "Papa," the name his grandchildren called him. They became his passion. For them, he was a frequent preschool guest class speaker, a high school football and water polo fan, a school concert regular attendee, a museum buddy, and a tour guide to his family in places as diverse as the Amazon in South America and his hometown of Philadelphia.

His children, and later his grandchildren, knew a Bernie who would dress up in silly clothes, tell goofy jokes, and splurge together on his favorite sweets, like birthday cake, ice cream, licorice, and Philadelphia pretzels. And, as he did as a child, he would regularly sneak them into a second movie at the multiplex.

We know of no other man who drank more fully of the essence of life. He savored world travel and learning, whether it be in school, by reading the encyclopedia, or by simply taking the time to get to know people from all walks of life. Even in his later years, he never stopped learning by reading, watching The History Channel, and seldom missing a new episode of *Jeopardy*.

Bernie was brilliant and caring, and he enjoyed teaching others. He never let fear quell an ambition nor silence what he needed to say, even when he was sharing an uncomfortable truth. "I have no regrets. I've done it all," he was fond of saying. He even chose to Bar Mitzvah in his eighties, since he had always identified strongly with his Jewish faith but had never experienced that right of passage as a teenager.

He was proud of what he had accomplished in life, and he let you know it. He loved being a plastic surgeon. He could be incredibly kind. He loved deeply, cared profoundly, and could be moved to tears. It gave him joy to help his fellow human beings, and his empathy fueled his passion to treat patients not only in his own practice but also in many remote and impoverished locations around the world.

People were drawn to Bernie by the magnetism of his personality. It would not be unusual to see him in the center of a crowd, be they friends or strangers, amusing them with stories of his adventures or misadventures—often using off-color humor that hinted at his childhood roots. He would often make us cringe, but we would also be smiling and often laughing.

Bernie died at home in March 2018. He was eighty-nine years old. For over twenty-five years he had fought to live, having overcome a heart attack, multiple strokes, diabetes, and two forms of cancer. His strength and love of life had always persevered until this point.

Even then, he was not ready to go, and he struggled at the end. However, he was surrounded by all of us who loved him. We were able to share our love during those last sad hours as we held him in our arms.

When the day of his funeral arrived, our immediate family was amazed at the number of people who joined us to pay their final respects. Doctors, whom Bernie had trained in the art of cosmetic surgery, flew in from all over the country. Many of his old office staff, nurses, and secretaries gathered at the chapel, reminiscing about the old days working for him. Friends and children of friends arrived, as did all of those wonderful people who helped care for him.

Bernie deeply loved this country and was proud of his service to it during the Korean War. He always wanted to have an honor guard present at his funeral, and this we were able to accomplish for him.

One soldier played "Taps" on his shiny brass bugle. The other stood stiffly in a silent salute as Bernard Koire, "Whitey's Kid," was laid to rest.

ABOUT THE AUTHOR

Dr. Bernard Louis Koire (1928 - 2018) was a noted plastic surgeon who practiced in Beverly Hills, California. He served in the Korean War and was buried with military honors.

www.ingramcontent.com/pod-product-compliance
Lightning Source LLC
Chambersburg PA
CBHW021623120626
46545CB00001B/364